FORTRESS
INTRODUCTION TO
AMERICAN JUDAISM

FORTRESS
INTRODUCTION TO AMERICAN JUDAISM

What the Books Say,

What the People Do

Jacob Neusner

Fortress Press ◇ Minneapolis

FORTRESS INTRODUCTION TO AMERICAN JUDAISM
What the Books Say, What the People Do

Photos are reprinted by permission of the following: Pages 58 and 76, Aliza Orent; Page 60, Lori Grinker; Pages 64 and 88, Aliza Orent and the Steiger family; Page 79, Dori Denelle Sterenson.

Scripture is from the Revised Standard Version of the Bible, copyright © 1946, 1952, 1971 by the Division of Christian Education of the National Council of Churches of Christ in the USA. Used by permission.

Cover design: Patricia Boman
Interior design: The Book Company/Wendy Calmenson

Library of Congress Cataloging-in-Publication Data

Neusner, Jacob 1932–
    The Fortress introduction to American Judaism : what the books say, what the people do / Jacob Neusner.
      p.   cm.
    Includes bibliographical references and index.
    ISBN 0-8006-2670-2 :
    1. Judaism—Social aspects—United States. 2. Judaism—Social aspects—Canada. 3. Judaism—United States—Customs and practices.
4. Judaism—Canada—Customs and practices. 5. Jewish way of life.
6. Judaism—20th century. 7. Sociology, Jewish. I. Title.
BM205.N483   1993
296'.0973—dc20   93-14856
                                                     CIP

Manufactured in the U.S.A.   AF 1-2670
98   97   96   95   94   1   2   3   4   5   6   7   8   9   10

CONTENTS

Preface   *vii*

Part I What the Books Say, What the People Do

Introduction   3

CHAPTER 1   The Puzzle of Describing a
            Contemporary Religion   13

CHAPTER 2   What the Jewish People in North America Do:
            Social Science's Portrait of Judaism   30

Part II   Why This?

CHAPTER 3   What the People Do in Synagogue: The Day
            of Atonement and Worship in the Synagogue
            on the High Holy Days   51

CHAPTER 4   What the People Do at Home: The Passover
            Seder and Hanukkah   63

CHAPTER 5   What Defines the Self-Evidence of the Judaic
            Rites of Passage? Circumcision, the Bar or Bat
            Mitzvah, Marriage, and Death   77

CHAPTER 6   The Judaism of Holocaust and Redemption:
            What It Is, Where It Governs   108

Part III   Why Not That?

CHAPTER 7   What Most Judaists Ignore—and Why   123

Part IV   So What?

CHAPTER 8   A General Theory of Why This, Not That, So What? With a Concluding Theological Postscript   153

Notes   166

General Index   175

Index of Biblical and Talmudic References   178

◇

This book introduces American Judaism—that is, the religion, Judaism, as it is practiced in America. It is a work concerned with the religion, Judaism, not with the sociology of the ethnic group, the Jews. Not all Jews are Judaists—practitioners of Judaism—although if and when Jews practice a religion, it is Judaism for the vast majority of them. And since most Jews at some occasion in their lives do practice Judaism, we study the religion from a very particular perspective: How, in America, do members of an ethnic group realize that they also wish to participate in a religious community, and how do they know whether they are only Jewish or also Judaic? That is the question I seek to answer in introducing American Judaism to readers concerned with the study of religion in general and religion in our own country in particular. Anyone interested in religion in general should study religion in the United States in particular, because, by all statistical measures, ours is a country that in higher proportions than most others claims to believe in God, Providence, reward and punishment, and afterlife, as well as weekly or even daily prayer. We have built in this country a nation with the soul of a church—but also a synagogue, as I shall show.[1]

When world religions come to America, they become American. Immigrants, whether from Africa or Europe or Asia or Latin America, bring with them nearly every religion known to humanity, and the immigrants and their children successfully naturalize not only themselves but their religions. Thus, no religion makes the move intact, but all of them come here ultimately unimpaired, and, given the profound measure of religiosity in this country, strengthened and renewed. In practicing a religion, why do people do certain things and refrain from doing other things within the norms of their religion? That question faces anyone who grasps—and everyone does—that religious elites write books, but ordinary folk embody religions, and therefore they know what counts and what doesn't. What do we learn from what they know about how religions work? My basic thesis is that, in its deep religiosity, America is a fundamentally Protestant country, and world religions that naturalize themselves here adopt the Protestant ethos for themselves. The reason is that Protestant Christianity solved the problem of religious diversity by privatizing religion, and for a country as diverse as our own, we have found no better way to civic amity and social stability than leaving people alone and, consequently, leaving religion to fend for itself as well. Just how this works for Judaism I spell out in this book.

In an earlier book, *The Enchantments of Judaism: Rites of Transformation from Birth through Death,*[2] I covered some of the same subjects that I treat here and asked the questions that I address here. In that book I asked how the rites of Judaism transform those who practice them—and why. The *how* part of my answer registered, the *why* part did not. Here I recapitulate the *why.*

In *The Enchantments of Judaism* one of the questions I sought to answer was, Why do people do certain religious deeds and neglect others? That seemed to me to be part of the question of religious transformation of the faithful (in the case of Judaism, sanctification). People took the title to mean that I was going to tell them how beautiful or how enchanting Judaism is. But to understand the book, one would have had to read it, not just flip the pages. So far as I saw, no general reviewer understood why the book offered, out of the case of Judaism, a proposition of general intelligibility on the character of religion as it lives and is practiced in North America (the United States and Canada).

I should not complain. The reviewers unanimously liked the book, which they thought was a nice introduction to the customs and ceremonies of Judaism: "enchantments" indeed! They missed the message of the subtitle, *Rites of Transformation*, not understanding that, to me, "transformation" stands for a question: How does it work? *Enchantments* quickly sold out in its commercial edition. But sales hardly justified a second printing. Not only so, but scholars in social science working on precisely the same problem did not realize that the book talked to them.[3] They never bothered to read a book about exotic Jewish customs and ceremonies—and they obviously did not follow the reviews. One looks in vain in the sociological studies cited in chapter 2 for a single reference to a work that addressed precisely the same question they propose to analyze—but from the perspective of the study of religion, and with special attention to the interplay between religious practice and theological norm. But then, for Jewish social science, ideas bear no weight, and theology is something they believe is absent in "Judaism" (or: the Judaism they study, weigh, and measure). Still, I wonder whether there is another field of learning so monumentally indifferent to reading books not bearing, in big red letters, the announcement, "This book is relevant to the work you are doing." That just might suffice to win the attention of Jewish social sciences to the contents of Judaism. The founders of social science spend their lives examining the tensions between the ideas people hold and the things they do; for Jewish social science, ideas do not exist; there is therefore no tension.

I should have preferred that the reviewers not like the book (even for all the wrong reasons) but at least understand it. And I should have hoped to inform, therefore also be informed by the response of colleagues in the social sciences. It would have been interesting to read reviews by scholars of the academic study of religion, but the book had not a single substantial review in a journal of religious studies, even though I worked within perfectly classical congeries of thinking. But we do not choose the colleagues with whom we share our field of study. In the world of Judaic learning even very friendly and loving reviewers do not read from the beginning to the end of a book—and in the Jewish social sciences even the best of the sociologists read only the raw data of opinion polls.

Still, I cannot plead guilty to focusing the book insufficiently, caring more for the atmosphere and nuance of language. I had the world's greatest editor, Phoebe Hoss, and writing for her approval meant a great deal to me. Even a superficial reading of *Enchantments* will show that I ask and answer a single question on every page of the book: Why this, not that? But the question is framed in context, the answer

teased out of the liturgy. Clearly, in casting as the generative question
of the book, How do the rites of Judaism change people? I chose the
wrong audience, expecting to address a world that is not asking the
questions I am answering—questions about religion, what it is, how it
works, illustrated by the case of Judaism. Jews who practice Judaism—
Judaists—are not going to want the answers; they already know them.
And Jews who study the Jews find religion implausible anyhow; so
there is no hearing there.

Here, therefore I re-present my theory to the audience to which I
should have addressed it to begin with: people who find religion important and want to understand religion in contemporary society, not
for believers who want nice stories about Jews' (exotic) customs and
ceremonies nor for the experts on the Jews and Judaism who like
collecting opinions but don't like reading books.

The issue that I addressed in the previous book and that is recast
for a broader audience of people who care about religion in general,
not Judaism in particular, is an urgent one: explaining what we see,
not only what we read. So I decided to rewrite the book and focus it
more sharply upon what strikes me as Judaism's most suggestive trait:
the fairly broadly diffused knowledge of what matters and what doesn't.
I have rewritten all of the chapters of that book for the purpose of
this one.

My dear friend and collaborator, Andrew M. Greeley of the University of Chicago and the University of Arizona and head of the
National Opinion Research Center, kindly read chapter 2 and gave me
the benefit of his learning and wisdom. He ranks among the nation's
most distinguished social scientists, in demography and ethnicity having
few peers, and I am proud of his friendship and thankful for the generous
gift of his time and knowledge. He knows the meaning of generosity
of spirit and of friendship and lives out the laws of collegiality.

The statistical description of American Judaism presented in chapter
2 derives from the works cited there. Many of the works I consulted
were located for me by Michael Satlow of the Jewish Theological
Seminary of America, who served as my research assistant. I consulted
also Jack Wertheimer of the Jewish Theological Seminary of America.
Manuscripts of his own public addresses were provided to me by Calvin
Goldscheider, Professor of Sociology and of Judaic Studies at Brown
University. For this help I thank all three.

As always, when working with Fortress Press I enjoyed the counsel of splendid editors, in particular Dr. Marshall Johnson. He saw the disorganization of the original draft and, in his own gentle way, suggested that I completely reorganize several of the chapters. I did so, with what I think is a good result. But he only exemplifies the high level of professionalism characteristic of that splendid press, with which I have been proud to be associated for nearly two decades now.

It remains to express my continuing thanks to the University of South Florida for providing ideal conditions in which to pursue my research, and to my colleagues in the Department of Religious Studies and in other departments for their ongoing friendship and stimulating conversation. They show me the true meaning of the word collegiality: honesty, generosity, sincerity. In my long career I have never known people of higher character and conscience.

I wrote this book while a Visiting Fellow at Clare Hall, Cambridge, among people whose ambition it is to make for scholars whatever in this world there can be of paradise. I cannot imagine a more congenial place in which to write a book or conduct intellectual experiments. The humble facilities of that research center conceal the wealth of spirit and intellect that flourish there; to the president and staff of Clare Hall and to the many friends and colleagues who accorded a warm welcome to my wife and me, I express thanks. Over thirty years now, a group of remarkable academicians, with much goodwill aforethought, conceived and brought into being a truly international community of scholars, encompassing humanities, social sciences, natural sciences, law and jurisprudence, and many other areas of learning, in which the resources of an ancient university would be made available to foreigners and indigenous alike. None of the many things that work well at Clare Hall is an accident.

Knowing, as I do, the current and former presidents of the college, recognizing the warm and constructive collegiality of the permanent fellows and the wonderful staff, I realize none of this is an accident. It is the result of hard work and deep thought about the nature of an academic community that really is a community. To my good friend, Clare Hall's President Anthony Low and to all his coworkers and colleagues I express my admiration and thanks for all that I have enjoyed on account of the work of these many men and women of goodwill but also effective wit. Being a veteran of a variety of research opportunities (more than a dozen research fellowships in national competitions of various kinds and thirty years of various university grants) and research institutes, I may say that everything they do wrong elsewhere they do right here.

It strikes me as providential that, at just the point in my life that I found, at the University of South Florida, a community of learning colleagues capable of genuine intellectual exchange and cordiality, I found here in Cambridge a similar community. Not many people know even one such place, and I know and enjoy a warm welcome in two of them.

Jacob Neusner

PART I

WHAT THE BOOKS SAY, WHAT THE PEOPLE DO

———————————————— ◇ ————————————————

This book introduces one of the world's religions in today's United States of America. Most, though not all, Americans say they are religious, and the world's religions flourish in today's America. In God most of us Americans really do trust. But each does so in his or her own special way, and that is what makes religion in America interesting. Religion is a native category for Americans, as the First Amendment makes explicit; and to understand America, we have to understand religion. What is at stake in the study of any particular religion in this country is the understanding of what happens to religion in America, and what we learn about America from how we practice our various religions here.

That is simply because most Americans are religious. They believe in God; they pray; they practice a religion; they explain what happens in their lives by appeal to God's will and word and work, and they form their ideal for the American nation by reference to the teachings of religion: "one nation, under God." This statement, from the Pledge of Allegiance, really describes how most Americans view our country. Americans act on their religious beliefs. Nearly all—upward of 92.5%—profess belief in God. A majority prays daily and weekly. A majority of Christians goes to church every week; nearly all Jews observe the Passover festival and most keep the Days of Awe (New Year, Day of

3

Atonement) and other religious celebrations. Religiosity is a fundamental trait of the American people and has been from the very beginning.

Most of the religions of the world are practiced in America. About 60% of the American people are Protestants (among them, 19% Baptists, 8% Methodists, 5% Lutherans, and the other 28% divided among many groups). Another 26% are Roman Catholics. About 2.5% are Jews, most of them practicing Judaism. Somewhat fewer than 1% practice Hinduism, and the same proportion, Buddhism. Only 7.5% of the American people profess no religion at all. It follows that we cannot understand America without making some sense of its diverse religious life. The marvel of America is its capacity to give a home to nearly every religion in the world, and the will of the American people to get along with one another, given the rich mixture of religions that flourish here. This book presents not only the better-known religions of America, Christianity and Judaism, but also the religious world of Native Americans, African Americans, Hispanic or Latin-American Americans, as well as the old religions newly arrived in this country, such as Islam (0.5% of the American people), Hinduism, and Buddhism.

Religion played a fundamental role in America's development by Europeans. The eastern part of this country was settled by people from Great Britain as an act of religion. The Southwest was founded by people from Spain and Latin America as an act of religion. Virginia and Massachusetts were founded by Protestants; Texas, New Mexico, Arizona, and California, by Roman Catholics. Other Roman Catholics, coming from Quebec, founded the first European settlements in the Midwest. New England is the creation of British Puritans from East Anglia; Virginia and the Chesapeake area, of British Anglicans (Episcopalians); Pennsylvania and New Jersey, British Quakers; and the Appalachian South, from West Virginia and western Pennsylvania south through Piedmont North and South Carolina, was established by British Presbyterians from the area around the Irish Sea, the border regions of Scotland and Northern England, and the Irish counties of Ulster, in particular.

The first European settlements in Texas, New Mexico, Arizona, and California were established by Roman Catholic missionaries and soldiers coming north from Mexico, who wanted to bring Christianity to the native peoples. Many of the place-names in the American southwest were given by Hispanic pioneers who acted in the name of Jesus Christ and the Roman Catholic faith. The earliest European explorers and settlers in the Midwest, from Detroit to New Orleans, were Roman Catholic missionaries and traders from Quebec, in French Canada.

From colonial times onward, many groups that joined in the adventure of building the American nation brought with them their religious hopes and founded in this country a particularly American expression of religions from all parts of the world: Africa, Asia, Europe, and Latin America. Entire American states and regions took shape because of religiously motivated groups, the Latter Day Saints ("Mormons") establishment of Utah and the intermountain West being one outstanding example. So ours is a fundamentally religious nation in which nearly every living religion is now represented in a significant way.

It is common to think of America as basically a Christian country because different forms of Christianity have predominated through America's history and have defined much of its culture and society. The vast majority of Americans who are religious—and that means most of us—are Christian. Is America therefore a Christian country? Yes, but not only Christian. To be a true American, one can hold another religion or no religion at all. The first religions of America were those of the Native Americans. And, while Protestant and Roman Catholic Christianity laid the foundations of American society, America had a Jewish community from nearly the beginning, the first synagogues dating back to the mid-seventeenth century. Today this country has become the meeting place for nearly all the living religions of the world, with the Zoroastrian, Shinto, Muslim, Buddhist, and Hindu religions well represented. Various religious groups from the Caribbean and from Africa and Latin America likewise flourish. Virtually every religion in the world is practiced by some Americans.

America is different, and we shall learn that Judaism in America is different from Judaism as it has ever been known, and as it is practiced everywhere else in the world today. The American difference is important to all America's religions. Other countries have difficulty dealing with more than a single skin color ("race"), or with more than a single religion or ethnic group, and modern nations split because of ethnic and religious differences. But America holds together because of the American ideal that anyone, of any race, creed, color, language, religion, gender or sexual orientation, or country of origin, can become a good

American under this nation's Constitution and Bill of Rights, its political institutions and social ideals. And while religions separate people from one another, shared religious attitudes, belief in God for instance, unite people as well.

America is different because—along with Native Americans—it has always been a land of immigrants. From its very beginning, but especially in the years since World War II, America has attracted people from everywhere. Today the great religious traditions of the world flourish in America, and many of them have become distinctively American. That brings us to the ancient and enduring faith of eternal Israel, the religion presented in the Torah, which the world calls Judaism.

Now to the thesis of this book in particular. By appeal to the character of American society and its reading of religion, I propose to explain the anomalies and ambiguities of Judaism as practiced in America. Religion answers urgent questions. Religion's answers find a hearing through their power to invoke the response. This is self-evidently true. Self-evidence is always social: we all know, we all concur. Then the answer matches the question, and religion governs the everyday. Therefore—with the perfect fit between answer and question—what the books say, the people do. Religion not only persuades; through the power of its truth it compels when the faithful hear the truth and recognize its self-evidence. But if the questions do not press, elegant answers go to waste. Truth competes not with falsehood but irrelevance. Answers no one needs, while true, prove self-evidently beside the point of life. So to ask, Why this, not that? we find out first what question is answered, and then find, among the answers that are heard, the common denominator.

That presents us with our theory, why this (which is heard, among the truths of the faith), not that (left in desuetude, among the same truths of the same faith). When we know what the books say—meaning in this case, the message of the liturgy and the meaning of the observance—we can identify the answer that is given. From the answer, we reconstruct the question that is answered. And from the streets and pews we assess what people hear. The sum of answers that find a hearing then derives from what the people do.

Let me state at the very outset the message of this book: Why this, not that? The rites of the Judaism actually practiced have in common a single trait: their focus on the individual, inclusive of the family. The rites of the received Judaism that for the generality of Jewry do not work speak to a whole society, or to civilization, to nation or people. The corporate community, doing things together and all at once, conducts worship as service. The corporate community celebrates and commemorates events in the world of creation, revelation, and redemption. Sabbaths and festivals focus upon the corporate life of Israel—a social entity. The words that people say on these occasions do not speak to many Jews. It is not because of lack of faith, but the absence of corporate experience of such a nature that would render plausible what is otherwise incredible.

For where people can refer comparable words to shared experience, namely, at home and with their families, working their way through life guided by rites of passage, their experience corresponds to the words they say, and they are changed by those words and want to be so changed by them. The individual rites of passage celebrating family, such as circumcision and marriage; and the rites that focus upon the individual and his or her existence, such as the Days of Awe, retain enormous power to move people. What speaks to the family on Passover—the home rite of the banquet—and moreover addresses the situation that the individual or family identifies as pertinent—resentment and remission—that component of Passover enjoys nearly universal response. The banquet symbol—matzah—imposes its spell, so that people who through the year and on Passover do not keep the dietary taboos do give up bread for the week and eat only matzah. At the same time, the synagogues on Passover contain plenty of empty seats. In my judgment, therefore, words work to make very private and personal worlds. Words do not work to create a corporate world of all Israel. In this collective denial of the public and the communal, the "we" gives way in favor of the "I," and that is what accounts for what people do and also for what they ignore.

The method of this book is simple. First we listen to the answer, then recover the question, of the rite. Only then, having taken up the contents, may we seek an explanation in the larger context of contemporary Judaism and so explain why this, not that. The same theory that tells us why people do one thing also explains why they do not do some other. So to ask the question: What basic theory, framed in the heart and soul of the religious life of Judaism, will explain the popularity of (for example) the Passover seder, which nearly everyone observes, and the neglect of the Sabbath, which nearly no one observes, and what moves people on the New Year and Day of Atonement, but not on the Festival of Tabernacles, following soon afterward? That question requires us to pay close attention to the liturgy. In this book the liturgy conveys what the books say, and the statistics of popular observance or lack of the same, what the people do.

Now, what the people do or believe may fall short of what the books say, or it may exceed the official norm, or it may just differ. But books rarely describe religions as the faithful believe in and practice them, and one can't gain knowledge of religion merely from books. How do we make sense of that fact? What do we learn about religion in today's world from the fact that believers negotiate, compromise, play the angles, and otherwise seem to know the difference between what God commands and what (in the framework of the faith to be sure) God will settle for.

Now the issue does not emerge when we contemplate our own religions. Jews who practice Judaism also know what (in their view) makes them "good Jews," and where they cross the line; Catholics know the self-evident rules that distinguish the normal from the fanatic; and even Mormons know when to laugh. But when we want to make sense of religion as we see it, our attention is drawn from what we know to what we need to understand, which is religions of other people: religion in general. How are we to proceed to follow the negotiations that guide the faithful—any group of faithful—across the gap between what the books tell them and what they choose to believe and do?

Here an analogy will serve to set forth both the problem and its solution. Studying about a religion other than our own is like learning a foreign language. We know one language, so we use that as a metaphor for all others; our American language provides the analogies that guide us in learning even utterly different languages. Any American who has studied French in books and spoken French in Paris knows the puzzle of studying Judaism in books and trying to make sense of Judaism in the workaday world—or Buddhism, or Hinduism, or Shinto, Tao, Islam, "native American religion," "the religions of Africa," "primitive religion," not to mention the religion of the Unification Church, the Mormons, Christian Science, the Catholics if we're Protestants, the Southern Baptists if we're Episcopalians, the Evangelicals if we're United Church, and so on. That is, we realize from our own experience in language that books about language give us the theory, but scarcely prepare us for the natural sounds of that language. In the case of religion, books about religion may well invent a religion in theory that scarcely exists in nature and in social fact.

That is why, while in books we learn what "the Jews believe," when we meet Jews in real life, we find that some believe this, some believe that, some believe everything, some nothing. Variations in religious practice, from the norms we learn in books, prove even wilder. Even the experts, such as the rabbis, may find surprising things that books tell us about Judaism, and that is not only because the books may err, but because rabbis too make things up as they go along. The tension between the received faith, portrayed in its canon, and the practiced faith, embodied in the imperfect learning and life of ordinary people (God's choice in priests, ministers, rabbis, imams, and all the rest is sometimes curious), proves ubiquitous.

The very construct "Judaism," with its beliefs and practices, simply ignores the complex and vital reality of the many Judaisms that flourish in the world, and that have existed in the past. Books really do mislead by taking the intellectual labor-saving devices of speaking of Judaism or Christianity or Islam, while the world in its natural state presents us with only Judaisms, Christianities, and Islams. And even if we know about the three main Judaisms of North America—Reform, Orthodox, and Conservative—we are not prepared for the remarkable range of differences among Jews of these denominations or sects, from Reform Jews who faithfully worship every Sabbath to Orthodox Jews who attend services on the Day of Atonement (but then wear the death shrouds that are de rigueur for the truly pious). How to solve this problem?

We can learn a foreign language in books and a foreign language as it lives in the streets, but it is only very recently that teaching foreign languages has aimed at introducing the living language. And, when it comes to the study of religion, we still invent what we teach to conform to an academic vision of the subject. Intellectuals seek order, sense in nonsense, so they naturally reduce things to patterns, of which they can make sense. But the work is to make sense of nonsense; to address religions in their natural condition so as to form generalizations concerning religion as it governs lives and the social order. Like the Japanese and Africans who, after years of study with expatriate British with impenetrable upper-class accents know and love Shakespeare but to the ears of Americans and ordinary Britons appear to be speaking Japanese, Swahili, or Zulu, so are the many Americans who, to make sense of the world, read books on religion and learn everything but what is really there. But as language teaching has progressed so that Americans arriving in Paris or Frankfurt or Stockholm after years of language study no longer are stunned to know no more than those who have not, so the study of religion can confront things as they are—and explain them.

In this book I invoke the case of Judaism as an example of the gap between book religion and lived religion. I offer a theory to account for the difference. By way of a working hypothesis I think I can say both why people do the things they do, as attested by a variety of social scientific surveys, and do not do the things they in general (leaving out only a tiny minority of perfectionists) neglect or dismiss or just ignore. And in explaining, for Judaism, the reason why and why not, I offer a theory of what it means to be religious in North America today. Since I take religion seriously and at face value, my theory invokes not only the out-there of the social world but the in-here of the message of faith and rite. I do think that the content of religion matters, not only its social form or utility. (As a faithful and practicing Jew, I even profess and live out the belief that God speaks to holy Israel in the Torah, which is why I spend nearly all of my working hours in the texts of the Torah.)

Why and how that works I shall explain in due course by showing that, within the received Judaism, some rites affect people and others do not. Stated simply, the question is this: Why do nearly all Jews attend the Passover banquet rite known as a seder, but the next morning only a few Jews then attend synagogue services in celebration of that same Passover festival? I believe I can answer that question in terms that illuminate the religious—and therefore also the political—life of Judaism and also Christianity in North America (therefore also much of Western Europe). But that encompassing theory becomes important only in its own place, at the end.

I shall also present a prescription for the reformation and restoration of the Judaic social polity—no small promise. But in studying about religion, we address the encompassing questions of society, culture, and politics, because religion answers in a cogent fundamental way the ineluctable questions of humanity in society, before God. Any picture of Judaism as a religion therefore takes its perspective from the proportion and composition of religion in general.

Let me state the problem in terms not only of religion within the social order but also of religion that infuses life with meaning and sanctifies the faithful. For when we study religion, we owe it to our subject to find language appropriate to what is at stake in the subject—appropriate to, and respectful of, the faith of faithful people. At issue in terms of believers (in this case, Judaism, but Christians in their framework surely can identify with what I say), is how religion transforms, how its rites enchant and change—and when, in the everyday world, religion fails to work its wonder. In these pages, there are the following premises.

The first is that words change things. Rightly spoken with proper intentionality, from the heart, words bring forth worlds, through enchantment turning the everyday into something remarkable. That is, through the enchantment of its rite, Judaism changes Jews from what we were into something else, something more, than what we had imagined. The enchantment takes place in heart and soul and mind, comes to expression in deed turned into gesture, and reaches fulfillment in the transformation of the here and now of the everyday into the then and there of life with the living God.

But, second, some words of Judaism work so as to make worlds of meaning only in a very particular circumstance, and that is, in the Judaism that thrives in North America, when words speak to the individual and to the family, when they pertain to the passage through life, or when they address an immediately felt experience. Lacking the experience of religion lived in corporate community, however, people find it difficult to enter into, let alone transform, those social worlds of Judaism that transcend the private life. When worlds speak of me, my life and my family, they transform; when they speak of us, all Israel, all together, in the language of the holy, the same words fall away unheard.

And, third, another set of words do work for those same Jews, words that make a different world from the one formed of imaginary Israel in the family of Abraham, Isaac, and Jacob. Those other words form a separate Judaism from the one evoked for individual and family on those rites of passage nearly universally observed. The corporate community unchanged by the words of one Judaism comes into being through the power of the words of a different Judaism. I identify that other Judaism and explain why in the context of the religious life of North America the nature of religion in general leads to the formation of two Judaisms that flourish today: one for the private life of home and family, the other for the political life of the community and its public policy.

In speaking of the power of words to form worlds, the strength of the imagination to define reality, I refer mainly to the liturgical life of Judaism: circumcision, the marriage ceremony (the huppah), the Passover banquet meal (the seder), the ineffable power of the prayers for the Days of Awe ("High Holy Days"). I examine the ideas expressed in these rites and ask why people say these words and are changed by them. I further invoke the equally moving liturgy of Sabbaths and festivals, and, above all, the Daily Prayer of the Shema, the Eighteen Benedictions. The same people deeply affected by some rites are left unmoved by others, as is shown by high levels of observance of some holy days but utter neglect of others (spelled out with statistics in chapter 2).

I try to explain why the former set of liturgies exercise power nearly universally, while the latter ones—Sabbaths and Daily Prayer—do not. In appealing to the contents of the liturgies of Judaism to explain why some rites enjoy currency and others decay, I treat as socially important the theological propositions of Judaism. I further maintain that the contents respond to the context as well. This analysis of the theological power of Judaism in its received form and of the presently definitive strength of a competing Judaism appeals to the interplay of contents and context, text and matrix. Yet the simple premise of this book is that the liturgy of Judaism *is* Judaism, so far as we understand by "Judaism" a religion comprising a worldview and a way of life formed in the discipline of God's will for humanity.

Judaism invokes imagination and the power of mind to construct a world, that is, Judaism rests on faith and conviction and trust, not merely on facts. Judaism also leaves Jews indifferent to its truths and rites. Here I propose to explain both the one and the other in such a way that people interested in generalizing about the workings of religion in the contemporary world may find a useful example of general intelligibility.

CHAPTER 1

The Puzzle of Describing a Contemporary Religion

◇

The books say one thing about a religion, the people who claim to believe in that religion say quite another. We, interested in the world about us in general and our neighbors' religions in particular, reading the books and living with the people, wonder why. Because religion defines the meaning of life for most people we know and shapes community life for many, bridging the gap between religion as described and religion as lived demands our attention. In fact, trying to understand the difference between official religion and believed and practiced religion defines a central problem in making sense of religion as we see it in today's world. Whether or not so considerable a gap in times past marked the space between the workaday believers and the official practices and beliefs, today, clearly, a labor of explanation awaits us: How do people know what to do, and what not to do, among the many things their religions prescribe? Apart from small circles of the truly and consistently pious, people do make choices about what counts and what does not, or, more to the point, what can be compromised or neglected, and what is going to matter.

I am not referring to sinning, for example, breaking the commandment "Thou shalt not commit adultery." That sinners sin is not a problem for the interpretation of religion, since the adulterer generally concedes that adultery does not accord with the religion he or she professes, and by the standards of that religion is wrong. I refer to compromises that leave the believer with a good conscience. Here is where religion lives but takes leave of the books in which it is preserved. By way of example I refer to Jews who keep the dietary laws at home but eat lobster when dining out, doing so in good conscience and with a fine rationalization. I mean, also, Catholics who practice birth control, Baptists who use liquor—and pretty much everybody else who, seeking to practice a perfect religion in an imperfect world manages the compromises that hold together conflicting demands, even so humble as a taste for shellfish or a desire not to have three dozen children.

What makes the problem interesting for the study of religion is simple: the same Catholic who practices birth control goes to confession and to Mass, and Baptists who drink beer Saturday night sing with a full voice and love of God Sunday morning, and Jews who eat unkosher food out keep two separate sets of dishes for meat and dairy products at home, and two more sets of dishes for Passover as well. There are also Jews who do not keep kosher at all during the year, but at Passover eat only Passover food and go so far as to get themselves kosher-for-Passover toothpaste and kosher-for-Passover furniture polish (intending, I imagine, to eat their dining room chairs). All of these choices make of religion something strange and wonderful, original and incomprehensible. But they also demand attention: How do we explain the difference? How do people know the difference between what is required and what—acceptably, amiably, with all the goodwill in the world—is actually done?

The stakes are high; the difference matters, because to make sense of the world, we have to understand something about religion: what it is, what it does, what people do, or do not do, because of it. And there is no more characteristic trait of religion than the abyss between what the books say about a religion and what the people do who practice and believe that religion. Or, more to the point, believers seem to know how to play across the gap between the faith as described and the faith as lived. But we are seldom let in on the secret of how they know. For, as a matter of fact, if we read books about religions, we acquire information that is accurate and even scholarly. But what we learn simply is not always relevant to what we learn about religions from everyday observation. Religions are ordinarily described so one-sidedly as ideal types that the description loses all contact with the everyday variations, not only within religions but between religions and believers of those religions. When we know one thing but see another, we have either to condemn what does not fit our knowledge, dismissing it as sinful or aberrational, or we have to consider a new fact in our framework and rethink what we know. In this book, through the case of Judaism, I propose a model for how to think about the gap between what books say about religion and what people do with religion.

Books that describe religions, written by believers themselves or by neutral scholars, do not prepare us for the kind of compromising and negotiating that at a subterranean level has to take place to accommodate what people are told they are supposed to do and what they will to do. Clearly, the faithful make choices. They do know answers to the question, Why this, not that? And they go a step further: So what? That is why, in the study of a particular religion in a particular time and place and circumstance, it is time for us to try to form a theory for the study of religion. I propose to explain, at least in one rather public case, why people practice the faith in some ways the way books say they do, in some ways not, and how they know the difference between what the books depict and what is all right to do anyhow. I shall give a very particular explanation for why American and Canadian Jews in general (omitting reference to statistically unimportant segments that are fully practicing and believing Orthodox) have made the choices they have made, and I shall tell why I think they have drawn the conclusions that they have drawn about what is fitting and what is dispensable.

But Judaism stands for only one case, an example of what I think is a generally familiar phenomenon. Every Catholic knows how to negotiate the difference between doctrine and what people really do. Everyone knows that the pope is in charge of the Catholic church; all the books say so. Anyone with Catholic friends knows otherwise, starting, for instance, with birth control. The pope says no, but most Catholics do what they want. Now we are dealing here not with papal authority concerning matters that the pope has no business directing, for instance, for whom Catholics will vote in an election. We are dealing with a matter of faith and practice to which the pope has devoted authoritative instruction. We learn nothing merely by condemning Catholics for using condoms or Jews who claim to be "traditional" for eating lobster and pork. True, we may well say that Jews are not really a religion but a mere ethnic group; or we may say that Catholics are hypocrites for using condoms. We will not understand them one bit better if that is our judgment. We should ask, by contrast, how it is that we know what we really do, as against what books or authorities say we do. When we put the answers together and analyze them, we will come to understand something about being religious in today's world. Dismissing with harsh—or, worse, condescending—judgment of other peoples' religious inconsistencies, while interesting, hardly helps us understand the world we live in, or the people with whom we share our country, or ourselves.

The everyday life of the world consists, in the end, of the results of negotiation and accommodation, and the human, workaday reality of religion, by which most people form and explain their lives, engages attention still more than the ideal picture of religion that books give us. How people negotiate teaches us about our humanity, and no mirror of humanity excels religion for a portrait of the human soul. We learn more about religion from how people do it than from the way books describe it. But without the heritage of learning to tell us the norms of the faith, we will not begin to know how to frame our question. So we require knowledge of both what books say and what people do. Then our task is to interpret each in relationship to the other, and that is what I shall do for Judaism in the United States and Canada.

In many ways, our problem in trying to understand religion runs parallel to the difficulty we have in understanding a foreign language. How many of us Americans, rarely hearing a foreign language and never having to use it except out of courtesy, have found that, after years of study, we can say little more than "Good morning," and then recite a classic poem the native speaker may never have learned? It is one thing to learn a language in a classroom, even read stories or newspapers in that language; it is quite another to use the language to communicate with a native speaker. Hearing about the language and mastering its rules scarcely prepares us for the natural sounds of that language. After four years of high school Spanish, unless you have the advantage of Spanish-speaking friends nearby who are willing to use the language naturally in your presence and with you, you cannot speak Spanish, understand it when it is spoken, or communicate in it in a natural way. You have learned the theory of the language, but not the language. And reciting Molière with a glistening accent will not get you a cup of coffee for breakfast in Tours, unless your host speaks English.

People who teach languages have long recognized this problem, and, in our own country at least, have worked to solve it. Contemporary language study addresses that problem with language laboratories, intensive stays in the foreign country, and other effective means to overcome the gap between, for one example, book German and real German as Germans live in the language (figure out on first hearing what your students mean when they tell you, "Zupah!" by which they mean what the British mean by "super" and you'll see the problem). Everyone understands that, in the end, the purpose of learning a language is to be able to use it, and a principal use is communicating in that language when one must.

When it comes to learning about religion, we have not yet bridged the gap between talk about religion, at which we excel, and affording a true grasp of a religion life, fully lived, which, in books and in our studies, we have yet to learn to do. If you know how to read the entire Hebrew Bible in the original, but cannot tell a Tel Aviv taxi driver where you want to go, you are in the same position as someone who knows all about (for instance) Buddhism but has never smelled the incense; about Southern Baptist churches, whether white or black, but never heard the singing; about Judaism, but never seen the Torah carried in its intricate choreography around the synagogue. Studying religion, by nature, involves reducing religious belief and practice, emotion and sentiment, to words; there is no choice. But words obscure, standing between ourselves and the thing we want to grasp. The word "sacrifice" for example, in the context of Judaism, does not convey the bloodiness of the rite; nor are only a few people shocked by the rite of circumcision, which is done out in the open, in full view of the community; nor by the Judaic rite of burial, which hides nothing: we shovel dirt on the coffin (or, in the state of Israel, on the merely shrouded corpse), and that is our religious duty. None of the full immediacy of religion comes to us in mere language. So in many ways, the books do their best, the people do the rest.

And yet, consider the alternative. Studying our neighbor's religions in books is the best way and, except for snippets of observations we may make from time to time (attending a christening or a bar mitzvah, for Episcopalians and Jews, for instance), the only way. To show the dilemma, a modest domestic example serves, again borrowed from the experience of studying a language. Both my wife and I have studied

Italian, she in the classroom, I, through everyday exposure on the streets of Italy, living among Italians and hearing the language. We both love everything Italian, but I would claim mine is a different love from hers; mine is less cerebral. For I understand a great deal of the Italian I hear; she cannot. When, at an international meeting, an Italian speaks the language slowly and clearly, I don't need the translation in the earphones; she does. But she can read *Pinocchio* in Italian; I stumble. I enjoy watching RAI's Italian news on cable TV; for her it is a trial. She can read the highly literate editorials of *La Repubblica* with ease; I do well with the headlines and short news stories about murder and adultery (my vocabulary for the streets is as specialized as hers for politics). She knows Italian grammar with great accuracy. I didn't know Italian had grammar. She once asked me a question concerning the use of the subjunctive, and I claimed, "Italian doesn't have a subjunctive"—until she said, well, what about *sarebbe*. Then I knew the answer to her question: "Oh, that . . . ! Well, this is what you say. . . ." Neither one of us knows Italian as the language should be known. Education gets in her way, ignorance in mine; I have too much confidence, she, too little experience. True, we both love everything Italian; but both of us miss something essential. So for the study of religion: if all we know is what we read, we miss the point; if all we know is what we see, there is no point.

The problem is still more complex because religions are rarely so simple, harmonious, or one-dimensional as book descriptions make them out to be. We all understand of course that, within the community of the faithful, differences of opinion flourish. But the conception of one Buddhism, one Islam, one Judaism, or one Christianity comes to us from the imagination of scholars. "Hinduism," for example, began in the imagination of the British, for whom it constituted a formation and a systematization of an entire world of cults and rites and communities. There is not now, nor has there ever been, only one "Judaism," single, unitary, standing in a linear relationship to one harmonious past; there have been only Judaic systems, formed out of a distinctive account of a worldview, a way of life, and a theory of what, or who, is "Israel," that is, the people of whom the Torah speaks. True, all Judaisms refer to the Torah (beginning with the Pentateuch). But each finds the verses congenial to its system, and the official writings, or the canon, take precedence over the convictions of the religious system. In theological terms, of course, all believers maintain that, however many Judaisms there may have been or now are, in fact there is only one true and authentic Judaism, which is theirs. That datum of theological conviction need not stand in our way in our search for an accurate description of "Judaism," and the same pertains to other religions. Take Christianity for one stunning example: anyone who describes a single Christianity, with lots of branches, using the language, "Christianity teaches" or "Christianity believes," portrays a world that never was, is not now, and never will be.

The books tell us about this religion and that religion, but each of those singular religions turns out in the real world to form a vast and quarrelsome family of related religions, Judaisms, Christianities, Buddhisms. Books define Judaism as believing in one God. And true, at the lowest common denominator, all Judaisms believe in one God. But knowing so general a fact hardly prepares us for the varieties of beliefs about God that perfectly faithful Jews maintain. We cannot understand their religion simply because we know its arithmetic.

So the problem with book religion is not merely its simplification (which cannot be avoided), but its formation of artificial constructs, categories that exist in theory but not in the social world. From what we learn about religion in what we read, there is an "it," a "thing," that we can define. "It" has beliefs and practices; it has a history; it teaches this and that; its believers do one thing but don't do another. And this formation of a made-up "it" presents us not with a simplification, but an outright distortion. We do not prepare people to understand what they see in the social world of religions, and even make it inevitable that they will misunderstand what they see and judge in all the wrong ways.

Book accounts of religion create expectations that conflict with observation, so people conclude (as in the case of Judaism) that the religion doesn't live, because they can't find what the books lead them to anticipate. This books do by spelling what an "it" teaches on God or ethics, narrating its (singular, harmonious, uniform) history, describing its "rituals," and telling its "myths." In these and other ways, we treat as uniform what is complex and diverse. Not only so, but our categories derive from our world, not that of the religion we address. So we invoke categories of description that make sense to us (e.g., history, ritual, myth, theology), and impose those categories on the realities of an alien com-

position that has its own distinctive categories. Thus a religion that has
no interest in history as we practice it is given a history, explaining in
terms of development and change what that religion describes and
explains in entirely other terms. Now, we need not apologize for doing
more than merely paraphrasing the other's story about the matter; the
work of independent minds is always to explain matters in a critical
spirit. But in this case the work of explanation distorts.

And yet, what choice do we have? When we describe and then
explain a religion wholly in terms of its own categories, we simply
paraphrase what it says, without trying to make sense of that religion
in terms that mean something to us. Then we can say what that strange
religion says, but in our world we speak gibberish. We convey no
meaning in our own behalf merely by saying the right words. We go
through the motions, like puppets. Then we are like a monkey typing,
or an elephant dancing. But when we describe and then explain a religion
wholly in terms of our own categories, we create a different kind of
confusion. Now we confuse our definition of religion with another
religion's definition of religion.

A concrete case derives from Christians' reading of Judaism, meaning, first, what they read about Judaism in books, and, second, what
they expect to see in the everyday life of Judaism. Books portray not
even an ideal type, but simply, a lifeless hulk; Christian expectations of
what Judaism should be derive from their conception of what religion
should be, and, quite naturally, they define religion out of the categories
of Christianity. But Judaism is not simply Christianity without Jesus
and the New Testament; it stands for different people, talking about
different things, to different people; it scarcely intersects, at the cate-
gorical level, with Christianity (though it has much in common with
the categories of Islam). Take religiosity, for instance. Christian piety
comes to expression in praying and singing; synagogue music in general
is lifeless. Christians think going to church every Sunday is the high
point of religion. Pious Jews pray in community to be sure, but piety
comes to expression in other, equally important ways—study of the
Torah, for instance. Christians do not think that God cares about what
they eat. Many Judaisms regard the act of eating as an occasion for
sanctification. Christians think that because Jews' rate of attendance at
synagogue weekly is much lower than Christians' attendance at church,
Judaism is not as strong a religion as Christianity, or they may even

conclude that Jews don't have a religion but are an ethnicity. Jews who observe the dietary laws think that since Christians eat anything, they'll do anything too. Here is a transaction in category deformation: we are thinking about the other wholly in terms of ourselves, creating in our own image what is in fact a monster.

Book religion presents problems not only when we read about other peoples' religions; it can also impede our understanding of the religion we call our own. The confusion of categories affects not only our understanding of religions other than our own. It impedes our under-standing—and experience—of our own religion. When, for example, secular categories enter into religious conversation, the result is pure chaos, mixtures of things that really do not mix. The point is so important to my larger argument that I digress and dwell on a striking example of how, when people confuse categories of religion, they lose the possibility of reading their own religious writings. The point is in three stages.

1. Book religion describes religion through highly intellectual lan-guage and categories. So if we want to understand the documents of our own religion not as statements of faith, but as religious documents pure and simple, we are going to read them as books tell us to.

2. But book religion can, and frequently does, focus upon what the religious documents might convey, not (necessarily) what they mean to say. Consequently, even when reading the religious writings of our own faith, when we read about them in the work of scholars and intellectuals—the ones who tell us "what the books say"—we are led in a direction other than the one that the writers of those religious writings wished to tell us to take.

3. And this leads to a category deformation, a confusion of categories, so complete that, in the end, we lose sight of what is belief and what is fact; we ask facts to attest to faith; and (much worse) we place faith under the judgment of secular facts.

Now this indictment of book religion is somewhat abstract, and to make it concrete, I turn to a case familiar to most Christians, this matter of the historical Jesus. By "the historical Jesus," people mean, the real man, who lived and taught and died, whom we know as we know other real men and women, which is to say, by evidence drawn from the past, read in accord with rules governing what is plausible about mortals in general. But no Christianity ever built its church on the foundation of an ordinary man, who lived and taught and died, but of a unique man, who rose from the dead. Then when, as a matter of theological inquiry, books portray "the historical Jesus," they ask a secular scientist or a historian to supply its facts so that we may negotiate issues of religious fact. When today's most prominent scholars of the historical Jesus tell us about their work, they promise facts of history, historically attained. But then they tell us that these facts pertain to what is only a quest for Christian faith, pure and simple. That is what I call a "category deformation," and I offer it as a fine instance of the difficulty in bridging the gap between what the books say and what the people do.

To understand how distorted is the representation of religion by books, I offer by way of prologue to my main case the following analogy: the Buddhists of the Orient decided that, after millennia of assuming that they knew, they wished to know who the Buddha really was, so they decided to investigate that question in accord with the rules of learning not in their religion but in physics, biology, and chemistry. They asked scientists to discover the bones of Buddha and investigate the physical property of his corpse. This, they decided, would tell them who, and what, Buddha really was. Unthinkable? Well, take the case of Christianity, the religion the people cherish by reason of God incarnate. Now, that same figure is to be defined and described not through the records of faith but despite them and against them. Historians, denying the premises of the faith at the outset, instruct the faithful about God incarnate. That the study of history tells us nothing about God (though, many would concur, its facts can instruct us in God's works) does not stand in the way of the book writers. Let me explain.

Until the nineteenth century, Christians took for granted that the figure we call "the Jesus of history," who really lived on earth, a fully human man, like all of us, and "the Christ of faith," that is, Christianity's Jesus Christ, God incarnate, entirely human, entirely divine, were one and the same. They also took for granted that the Gospels, properly understood, tell us about Jesus Christ on earth. But in the earlier part of the nineteenth century, a different reading of the Gospels, drawing upon premises other than those of historic Christianity, that of Liberal Protestant theologians, particularly in Germany, differentiated between the Jesus of history and the Christ of faith. Not only so, but scholars working in universities and claiming to speak not gospel truth but historical fact promised to present the historical facts about the man, Jesus. These facts would belong in the same category as all other facts of history and would be formulated by the same rules, on the basis of the same reading of evidence. In consequence, over the past two hundred years, intense historical study has addressed to the Gospels a secular agendum grounded in three premises: (1) historical facts, unmediated by tradition, themselves bear theological consequence, the gift of the Reformation (only Scripture, so show me as fact in the sources); (2) historical facts must undergo a rigorous test of skepticism, the donation of the Enlightenment (how could a whale swallow Jonah, and what else did the whale have for lunch that day?); and (3) historical facts cannot comprise supernatural events, the present of nineteenth-century German historical learning ("exactly how things were" cannot include rising from the dead, which, after all, violates the rules of nature and is meant to!).

But this kind of historical study brought to bear upon the Gospels a set of premises that, to begin with, violated the character of the Gospels, as much as physics, chemistry, and biology cannot tell us the composition of Buddha. It has been a long-term confusion of categories—secular historical ones imposed upon a profoundly religious writing; so too, there has been a mixture of purposes, a historical quest for facts to settle theological debates. These premises set a standard of historicity that religious writings that set forth a religious faith, such as the Gospels, cannot, and should not, attempt to meet. For, after all, all three givens dismiss what to the evangelists is critical: these things happened in the way the church has preserved them in the Gospels, tradition being a valid source; these things really did happen as the narrative says (would the Gospels lie?); and Jesus Christ assuredly performed miracles in his lifetime and rose from the dead (ours is the story of the unique man, God among us). The quest for the historical Jesus commences with the denial of the facticity of the Gospels in favor of their (sometime, somewhere) historicity. So to begin with, the quest of the historical Jesus, from the Life of Jesus movement in the middle of the nineteenth century forward, has laid theological issues before the tribunal of secular history, and theologians thought to establish historical facts to settle theological questions.

Now, in point of fact, the confusion of categories masked a great clarity: in fact, the quest for the historical Jesus was and remains an entirely theological inquiry. Answering the question, Why bother? John P. Meier, in his *A Marginal Jew: Rethinking the Historical Jesus*, forthrightly responds in this-worldly terms: "The quest for the historical Jesus can be very useful if one is asking about faith seeking understanding, i.e., theology, in a contemporary context.... Faith in Christ today must be able to reflect on itself systematically in a way that will allow an appropriation of the quest for the historical Jesus into theology." This is for four reasons. First, "the quest for the historical Jesus reminds Christians that faith in Christ is not just a vague existential attitude or a way of being in the world. Christian faith is the affirmation of and adherence to a particular person who said and did particular things in a particular time and place in human history. Second, the quest affirms that the risen Jesus is the same person who lived and died as a Jew ... a person as truly and fully human ... as any other human being. Third, the quest for the historical Jesus ... has tended to emphasize the embarrassing, nonconformist aspects of Jesus.... Fourth, the historical Jesus subverts not just some ideologies but all ideologies...." And, he concludes, "the historical Jesus is a bulwark against the reduction of Christian faith ... to 'relevant' ideology of any stripe. His refusal to be held fast by any given school of thought is what drives theologians onward into new paths; hence the historical Jesus remains a constant stimulus to theological renewal."

Now, with the best will in the world, these apologia strike me as nothing other than constructive theology masquerading as history and in the name of a healthy religious intellect claiming the authority of reasoned, historical scholarship. Replacing theology as the arbiter of truth, history is given a weight hardly justified by even the pertinence of its methods—or even of its premises. These, in context, are simply irrelevant to what is subject to discussion. Why ask history to settle questions that Meier himself specifies as fundamentally religious, matters of not fact but faith? And since when do matters of fact have any bearing on the truths of faith? Real historians do not give reasons such as these for writing, for example, lives of Hitler and Stalin; I look in vain in Allan Bullock's *Parallel Lives* for a counterpart to Meier's (and

Crossan's) explanation of their lives of Jesus, and the comparison between his explanation of his work and theirs of their biographies leaves no doubt that his is a historical, theirs a theological, agendum, pure and simple.

John Dominic Crossan, in *The Historical Jesus: The Life of a Mediterranean Jewish Peasant,* presents an equally theological answer to the question, why look for Jesus in history: "This book . . . is a scholarly reconstruction of the historical Jesus. And if one were to accept its formal methods and even their material investments, one could surely offer divergent interpretative conclusions about the reconstructible historical Jesus. But one cannot dismiss it or the search for the historical Jesus as mere reconstruction, as if reconstruction invalidated somehow the entire project. Because there is only reconstruction. For a believing Christian both the life of the Word of God and the test of the Word of God are like a graded process of historical reconstruction. . . . If you cannot believe in something produced by reconstruction, you may have nothing left to believe in." Indeed. That proves my point: history in form, theology in substance, intent, and result.

I dwell on this example because it is a commonplace one and shows how much damage we do when we use the wrong tools in shaping our understanding of matters. And the wrong tools are manufactured by the excessive reliance upon philosophical abstract untempered by detailed observation—social science without statistics, physics in the mind. That is not to suggest "religions" do not "believe" things or practice them. It is to say, an adequate description of a religion moves beyond the binding of a book. The norms of a religion, which set forth the framework of description, have to make their peace, too, with the facts of religious belief and practice among the faithful. Rarely are they the same, in one place, for very long: that is the glory of the story of religion.

So when I compare studying a religion other than our own to studying a foreign language, it is to show the gap between book learning and street learning, and to explain what is at stake in these pages: to show how to play over (not around) the gap. The books organize things one way, the people who believe and live the religion, in some other way. The books do not prepare us to grasp what we are seeing. It becomes our task to make sense of such nonsense: what tells people what is "really" necessary, among the many things that are right? How do we explain to ourselves both why people do not do the things they dismiss, and also why they do the things they deem essential? The answers to these questions draw us deep into the territory of the everyday, because what we are trying to make sense of is common sense. And there, the facts of the quotidian life, the social order people perceive and embody, come into play.

Shall we then turn our description of religion into a labor of (mere) demography, defining Jesus Christ by appeal to how people this morning imagine him to be, defining "Judaism" or the Torah by examining the conduct of Mrs. Goldberg in Brooklyn, not to mention her daughter, Mrs. Sullivan in White Plains? Resolving matters in favor of the streets vastly misstates the power of the scribes. For if all we have in hand are the impressions we form of our neighbors' religion from their practice of it, we also cannot make much sense of matters. For my argument I appeal once more to the analogy of learning a language. As I write these words, I am starting my Swedish lessons, since I shall spend a semester in a Swedish-language university in Finland and wish to use the occasion as an opportunity to learn some of the language. In prior trips to Scandinavia I mastered the word for "Thank you" in Norwegian, Swedish, Danish, and Finnish (that one took two weeks!)—but not much more. I had no way of sorting out the natural sounds of the language. By contrast, after a year of Portuguese, while not exactly fluent, I could vastly improve my knowledge of the language in Brazil, and the same was so for Spanish in Madrid. Not knowing anything, you don't learn much; knowing the grammar, you learn much.

Try learning a foreign language without knowing any grammar. It can be done, but it takes years, and leaves vast gaps. Try explaining "Judaism" out of the data of your Jewish neighbor's practices. What you learn may be so specific as to prove unrepresentative, therefore useless. All you know when you meet a Jew other than your neighbor is that the next Jew's Judaism is like that of your neighbor in this way, but unlike it in that. So you have to have a theory of the religion, but you also have to frame a theory in response to the religion as it lives today, in the here and now that you are likely to encounter and want to understand. But then try to describe Judaism by reading a public opinion poll of belief and practice in the United States and Canada. What you learn is how people have modulated or modified or made their peace with something of which you are utterly uninformed: a plebiscite, where they forgot to put the proposition on the ballot. "Yes" or "no" votes do not inform. To understand what people do, you have to know the choices they have made, the processes of thought they have undertaken but also encountered—their own, those of the holy books they study, of the holy people they cherish. Religion in the instance of Judaism is a centuries-long process of negotiation between the dead and the living because the dead never die but live in the generations to come. No religion relies more heavily than Judaism upon the family, the mother and the father and those before; nor does any construct more weighty a structure upon the foundation of the social entity ("Israel" in its correct sense, the holy people of whom the Torah speaks, comprised here and now by "us"). It is then less a theology than a genealogy—but a genealogy accessible through theology, since, after all, people become "Israel" through religious conversion. So neither Mrs. Goldberg nor Mrs. Sullivan tells the whole story; I only argue that they tell an important part of it, even if (as in the case of Mrs. Sullivan, Mrs. Goldberg's daughter) probably the last chapter for that Goldberg family.

At this point you may legitimately ask, what's at stake? For describing religion and trying to explain to ourselves its power in human affairs, everything is at stake. Let me again invoke the analogy of language study. In the case of learning a foreign language, at stake is access to the world beyond the language curtain that falls in front of us as soon as we set foot in a non-English-speaking world. But while we can live behind our own language curtain, we cannot make sense of the world solely within the framework of our own religion, or the representation of religion we see hereabouts. When I taught in Germany, I taught in German, at heavy cost to intelligibility and expression; I owed the students that much. The one class I taught in my entire life in the state of Israel I presented in Hebrew, though my accent makes me sound as though I descended from the moon that morning. I wanted to pass through the language curtain, so that what I wished the students to learn would reach them in their own language and idiom (if in a slightly strange accent). Language is the passport to the rest of humanity; the visas are many, and you never have enough. But there is no entry into another world without mastering the words and the grammar that make them into sentences. The facts of religion are its vocabulary; these we learn in books but also in the streets. The grammar of religion is its holy writings, and these we learn in books. And the morphology, structure, principles of intelligibility (what you can and cannot say, to whom, and where and when)—these we learn in the speaking of the language, or in the here-and-now living out of the religion.

In fact when it comes to studying about religion, the stakes are very high—higher than studying a language. Most of us have little use of foreign languages; if we go abroad, it is for brief visits; we scarcely hear foreign languages at home, and, when we do, it is from Americans like ourselves, who also speak English. Rarely must we speak a foreign language, still more rarely is there no alternative. And even English-speaking Canadians in Quebec can take for granted that most people they meet know English (a presumption the Francophone Canadians may not appreciate). But in learning about religions other than our own, what is at stake is understanding most of the world beyond our home and family and neighborhood or barrio, and, in an American society where marriage among people of different religions is routine, within as well. Not only so, but since we live in a Protestant Christian majority, people other than mainline Protestants, not to mention Catholics and Jews, have to make some sense of the diversity of what they would prefer to classify as one, uniform "Protestantism," and everybody who opens a newspaper is required to make sense of Islam, not in its theory as a uniform and unanimous community of the faithful, but in its reality as diverse. With the advent, in the United States and Canada, of large numbers of the faithful of religions that flourish in the Caribbean and South and East Asia, moreover, knowing something about religions identified with Americans of European origin hardly suffices any longer.

Not only so, but for Christians the very notion of a "religion of our own" challenges perceived reality. Faced with the choice, "What is that religion that is your 'own' religion—Judaism, Christianity, Buddhism...?" Christians naturally check Christianity. But asked, What is your religion? the answer is more likely to be "Southern Baptist" than "Christian." Indeed, the single most complex and changing religion in the world today must be that construct of theology, "Christianity," with the remarkable development of Evangelical Christianity in Latin America and among Hispanic Americans in the United States; the confrontation of Catholic Christianity and Islam in Africa; the rebirth of rivalries among Christianities in Yugoslavia, the Ukraine, and Russia; the reentry of Christianity onto center stage after something more than a century of mere, stable respectability. People now fight wars for or against religion, and Christian armies facing Muslim ones no longer come to us only on the pages of history books. In the most recent past, "Onward, Christian Soldiers" was a battle hymn that would have served in Lebanon. So when Christians tell us they are studying "their own" religion, whether in a course on the New Testament or in one on "Christian theology," they represent a subject that is as misrepresentative as the one portrayed in books on Basic Judaism or What the Jews Believe.

So we use the case of Judaism as an example of playing across the gap between ideal and reality, the discontinuity between books and streets, the conflict between compelling theology and the indifferent facts of religious faith and life. What I owe is a theory of why this, not that, so what? That is, can I explain why Jews do the things they do, and, by reference to that same theory, can I also account for why Jews do not do the things within the same religion—the Torah—that they choose not to do? And, finally, can I spell out a theory for the character and working of religion in North America—the United States and Canada—so that, out of the exemplary facts of Judaism, we learn something about how religion works in our shared society? If I can, and I shall try to do so, then I shall have helped people make better sense of the here and now, and perhaps, too, able to shape the future. For that is what is always at stake in our making sense of so powerful, so protean a force as religion in society: the shaping of the future.

What the Jewish People
in North America Do

Social Science's Portrait of Judaism

◇

The Jews in the United States form an ethnic group, meaning, a group that bears in common certain indicative traits of behavior and conduct, origin and outlook. Many of the members of the Jewish ethnic group also practice the religion Judaism. Judaism is the religion of one people, because, by its own theology, when a person adopts the faith of Judaism and its way of life and worldview, that person also enters into the social entity "Israel," meaning, in Judaism, the holy people, God's first love, to whom the Torah is revealed; but meaning, in the common life, the Jews, or, more recently, the state of Israel in the Land of Israel. Consequently, we deal with ambiguity when we speak of the Jews and Judaism and the various senses and meanings of "Israel" that circulate, quite properly, among them and in the world at large. But there is no Judaism without real people, practicing a living faith, and since the people who practice Judaism are not only Judaists but also, by definition, Jews, in trying to describe the lived and practiced religion, Judaism, in America, we find ourselves at the boundary between religion and society.

In introducing into the study of Judaism the facts of everyday social life, I locate my inquiry within the framework of the study of religion and society. I ask how religious beliefs come to realization in the social order, and how (reciprocally) the social order takes shape in response to religious beliefs. Since we manifestly observe that different Jews do different things in the name of one and the same Judaism, we have to account for not only different patterns of social behavior, but also different Judaisms. That explains why the approach I work out here requires us to describe not one, unitary Judaism as a whole (which, in our time, exists only in the imagination of theologians or philosophers or ideologues, for whom the construct "Judaism" bears heavy meaning or, at least, saves a great deal of mental labor), but *a Judaism*. By "a Judaism" I mean a religious system, comparable in its constitutive components to any other religious system but distinctive in its particular mythic and symbolic traits.

"A Judaic religious system," like any other religious system, then is composed of three elements: a worldview, a way of life, and a (theory of the) social group that, in the here and now, embodies the whole. The worldview explains the life of the group, in the instance of a Judaism ordinarily referring to God's creation, the revelation of the Torah, the goal and end of the group's life in the end of time. The way of life defines what is special about the life of the group, in the case of a Judaism, what sanctifies the people, Israel. The social group, in a single place and time, then forms the living witness and testimony to the system as a whole and finds in the system ample explanation for its very being. That is *a Judaism*.

How shall we know when we have a Judaism? The answer to that question draws us to the data—the facts—we must locate, describe, analyze, and interpret. All Judaisms appeal to the Torah as the complete and exhaustive account of God's will and word for the world. Judaisms differ on the contents of the Torah—the books that belong to the canon.

The first requirement in identifying a Judaism is to find a group of Jews who see themselves as "Israel," that is, the Jewish People who form the family and children of Abraham, Isaac, Jacob, Sarah, Rebecca, Leah, and Rachel, the founding fathers and mothers. That same group must tell us that it uniquely constitutes "Israel," not *an* Israel, the descriptive term we use. Then, but only then, we have believers: (a) Judaism that is (to them) Judaism: "Israel" here and now and uniquely. A Judaism, or a Judaic system, is not a book that talks about this and that; it is a social group that appeals, also, to a book, to define its worldview and its way of life. When we study a Judaism, we are not studying a problem of intellect, but a circumstance of a social group in its intellectual formation.

The second point of analysis draws our attention to the group's social behavior: the facts of distinctive action that make the group special not only in mind, but in manner. The received holy books set forth a long menu of requirements. A given "Israel" will know which, among them, matter, and how these are to be done: the way of life.

The third requirement is to identify the forms through which that distinct group expresses its worldview. Ordinarily, we find that expression in writing, so we turn to the authoritative holy books that the group studies and deems God given, that is, the group's Torah or statement of God's revelation to Israel. Since we use the word Torah to mean biblical books, starting with the Five Books of Moses (Genesis, Exodus, Leviticus, Numbers, and Deuteronomy), we must remind ourselves that the contents of the Torah have varied from one Judaism to the next. Some groups regard as holy what other groups reject or ignore. A more suitable word than Torah, therefore, is canon, meaning the collection of authoritative writings. The canon contains much of the group's worldview and describes its way of life.

We of course err—and that is by definition—if we treat as our sole source of facts only what is in writing. And that explains the problem of this book: how to describe both what we know in books and what we observe in the streets. I maintain that in North America, while many Judaisms flourish, when we examine the conduct of masses of people, we can legitimately claim to describe one Judaism, to which most Judaists—practitioners of (a) Judaism—adhere.

The distinction just now introduced, between Jews and Judaists, requires explanation. Anyone born of a Jewish mother is a Jew according to the definition given in the Talmud. But not all Jews by such a definition—children of Jewish mothers—may be said to practice Judaism. By their own word, a fair number of Jews regard themselves as Jews by ethnic identification but not by religious belief and practice. Some children of Jewish mothers practice Christianity or Islam or Buddhism. They remain Jews, but they are not Judaists. No definition of "Israel" can exclude them, but none can accord them an honorable position either. Theologically, they are apostates; sociologically, they may or may not find a place in the ethnic entity, "the Jews"; some want, some don't want, to belong to that. Although they no longer have any connection to Judaism, whenever they wish, without a formal act of affiliation or conversion, they may resume that connection.

That explains why, in order for us to study the religion, Judaism, we have to distinguish between ethnic Jews and religious Jews, whom we call practitioners of Judaism or "Judaists." An ethnic Jew may take an active role in the organized political life of the Jewish community (as may the non-Jewish spouse of a Jew); but such a person does not claim to believe in or practice Judaism. If we wish to study Judaism as it is practiced (or more accurately, Judaisms as they are practiced), we shall have to accept such persons at their word and regard them as secular, telling us nothing about the religion, Judaism. So far as statistical descriptions of Judaism distinguish between the Jew who professes Judaism and the Jew who does not, we shall describe only the Judaism of the Judaist and ignore those who identify themselves as an ethnic group but not a religion, for they provide no facts on Judaic belief and behavior in North America. We have substantial evidence concerning a massive Judaism, dominant among the Judaisms of the United States and Canada, evidence that derives from social scientific surveys of Jews' beliefs and behavior. A full, well-documented definition of the Judaism at hand emerges in these pages.

A Judaist, whether Reform, Orthodox, humanist, Reconstructionist, Conservative, or an adherent of any of the other Judaisms, is also a Jew by definition, since one becomes a Jew through Judaism (religious conversion), an ambiguity not to be ignored. A Jew becomes a Judaist without conversion, by the act of identification with a Judaism, through some routinely recognized gesture. A Judaist born of a gentile mother also is automatically a Jew. Admittedly, ethnic Jews, defining themselves as they do by ethnic origin, do not always receive a warm welcome, because naturalization is effected into the ethnic group through adoption of attitudes or tastes deemed generally definitive but rarely defined for the convenience of the postulant.

Why in the description of Judaism do the books conflict with the behavior of the people? Should it not suffice to say, the books say this, but people sin and do that? It would if matters were so simple. But the point of conflict between books and behavior lies not at the interstices between normative conviction and aberrational conduct. It is between the premises of the books and the social platform of the living community. In the surveys before us, we shall note that the sociologists report a simple fact: people think they are "good Jews" who keep one holiday and ignore another, observe one rite and neglect another. It is that conception of the self-evidence of what people do and do not do, within the repertoire of choices made available to them by the holy books they revere that requires analysis and explanation. What accounts for the self-evident necessity of one thing but the obvious excess of another? All of this will become clear below.

To begin with, Judaisms address the social situation of the Jews that embody those Judaisms; Judaisms take for granted a given circumstance and address the issues implicit in that circumstance. The fundamental discontinuity between the holy books of Judaism and the social situation of North American Jews is the premise of the books that Jews are holy, that means, sanctified and separate from everybody else; the premise of the social world of Jewry in North America is the opposite: Jews are not separate from everybody else except in some ways—ways they choose. Everything else rests on that remarkable disjuncture between the imagined social world of the holy books and the chosen social world of the people who read and respond to those books.

The parting of the ways between the books and the faithful people may be stated thus: the holy books of Judaism speak to people who are always and only Jews. Moreover they are Jews by God's choice, subject to an eternal covenant between God and Israel, which they cannot abrogate but may only violate. But the social platform of American and Canadian Jews rests on the principle that Jews are also Americans or Canadians, integrated by choice, not segregated by choice. They suffer no obligations except those they voluntarily accept; and a votive obligation is an oxymoron. "Israel" is Israel because a person feels like it, wants it, affirms it, always voluntarily; never coerced by God, on the one side, or by a hostile society, on the other (or even by a friendly and welcoming society for that matter). And at that point, the books become simply implausible; they speak of an "Israel" no one knows, or wants to comprise. To people who may choose to be Jews or may decide to live only among Jews or to live with Gentiles as well, books that speak only of holy Israel, a people that dwells apart, deliver a puzzling message, one to be negotiated and affirmed but also interpreted.

Books did not always present the faithful with implausible premises. It is a matter of simple fact that for a very long time, from late antiquity to the eighteenth century, a single Judaism predominated, a Judaism that took for granted that Jews were always and solely "Israel," defining the social entity "Israel" as against the nations. No provision, in such a Judaism, accommodated what we may call integrationism: the desire to be Jewish but something else in addition; nor did that Judaism and its holy books distinguish the ethnic from the religious. During this long period, the principal question facing Jews was how to explain the success of the successor religions, Christianity, which claimed to replace the Judaism of Sinai with a new testament, and Islam, which claimed to replace it with a final and perfect prophecy. Both religions affirmed but then claimed to succeed Judaism, and the Judaism of the dual Torah enjoyed success among Jews, allowing them to make sense of the then-subordinated status of the enduring people and faith of Sinai.

While during this long period heresies took shape, the beliefs of the new systems responded to the structure of the established one, so that a principal doctrine, for example, the doctrine of the dual Torah, written and oral, or of the Messiah as a faithful sage, would take shape in opposition to the authoritative doctrines of the Judaism of the dual Torah. For our purposes what counts is that this Judaism defined the way of life and worldview of its "Israel" without ever assuming that its "Israel" would become something else in addition, such as "American" or "Yankee fan."

In the nineteenth and twentieth centuries, continuator and successor Judaisms came into being, such as Reform and integrationist-Orthodoxy as an articulated Judaism, and the like. The principal question addressed by new systems that drew upon the books of the received one concerned matters other than those found urgent by the received Judaism of the dual Torah, with its powerful explanation of the Jews' status in the divine economy. The particular points of stress, the self-evident answers to urgent questions, came at the interstices of individual life. Specifically, Jews needed to explain to themselves how as individuals able to make free choices on their own, they found a place within the commanded realm of the holy way of life and worldview of the Torah of Judaism. The issue again was political, but it concerned not the group but the individual. Judaisms produced in modern times answered the urgent question of individual citizenship, just as the Judaism of the long period of Christian and Muslim hegemony in Europe, Africa, and Western Asia had taken up the (then equally pressing) question of a subordinated but (in its own view) holy society's standing and status as Israel in Islam or in Christendom. So much for what the books say, and to whom they say it. What about the people and what they do?

In order to know what people do we must ask questions. Social science, particularly the demographic wing of sociology, through its mastery of correct polling techniques and of statistics, provides a generally reliable account of how people describe their behavior. True, opinion polling produces its embarrassments, as 1948's "President Dewey" can testify. But, tested over decades, demography—the statistical description of social behavior—has shown itself accurate. Not only so, but, for our purposes, we ask for broad gauged percentages, drawing conclusions when most people do one thing but not some other, for example, 90% do this, and 90% do not do that. In such an instance, we are able to test the impressions of the naked eye against the statistics of surveys and vice versa, asking for nothing so close as a 2% range of possible error.

Relying on social science for the study of religious behavior, of course, hands over to a profoundly (and properly) secular field the interests of a deeply religious one. I am referring not to a secular and unbelieving attitude as against a faithful and devoted one but to the very selection of data for examination. Most of the questions sociologists ask concern the makeup of society, how old people are, where and with whom they live, who their friends are, what they do for a living, how much they make, and the like. Along the way, questions that tangentially interest the students of religion come up: Are they married to a Jew or a Gentile? Do they belong to a synagogue? give to a Jewish charity? keep dietary taboos? attend synagogue? and the like. All of the questions sociologists raise concerning religious behavior and belief bear on the prior interests of sociologists in social behavior.

But a range of questions interests us that sociologists do not include in their questionnaire: How is the rite of circumcision performed? by a doctor or a ritual specialist? Who is called upon to bury the dead and where are they buried? Who performs the marriage between two Jews, a rabbi or a justice of the peace? The questions lead us deep into the formation of a Judaism by popular behavior, but have no profound bearing on the description of the social order. Sociologists ask them, only when engaged in a detailed study of a well-delineated religious group (Orthodox or Conservative Jews) if they ask at all. But when describing the Jews at large, these questions do not yield differentiating data and therefore are not asked. If, by contrast, we want to know about what the people do, as against what the books say, we have a much longer agenda of issues, defined for us by the books, disposed for us by the people. Time and again, in the chapters that follow, I shall have to say, I could find no current data.[1] The task at hand—contrasting what the books say with what the people do—begins with the recognition that our data derive from a field of learning that by definition dismisses as irrelevant what books say.

Let me now proceed to the task of the social description of Judaism as practiced in the United States and Canada. For our purposes of describing the generality of Jews' conduct in religious matters, I present figures that outline a broad consensus, excluding only the fringes. These are in two directions. On the one side are the total integrationists, on the far side of Reform Judaism, who retain only a residual connection with Judaism by reason of birth (and, if male, circumcision) but who have opted out of Jewry. Such people locate themselves out of reach of social scientific study because there is no way of identifying them by any actions generally defined as Judaic in character, for example, synagogue attendance; or as Jewish in ethnicity, for example, giving money to a Jewish charity or supporting the state of Israel in politics. It is not for us to declare them no longer Jews; but in any study of Judaism as a religion, they do not wish to be included and so the data they provide concern the sociology of Jewry but not the morphology of Judaism. On the other side are the total segregations, on the far side of Orthodox Judaism, who have chosen to live as far as they can outside the framework of American life. Their Judaism is not described in accounts of the generality of American Jews, because they form too small a percentage to matter.

The issue of the contrast between books' description and peoples' behavior emerges when we examine the behavior of that vast middle, encompassing the different Judaisms of North America, the best known being Reform, Orthodox, Reconstructionist, and Conservative (although there are many others). These are the Jews who cherish the books but also form a pattern of measurable behavior clearly different in some ways from what the books describe as the Judaic way of behaving, and who profess beliefs not entirely (or even very little) shaped within the lessons of those books. They form the problem: how do we play across the gap between books and behavior when we study religion? To state what I think is at issue for that huge middle, encompassing better than 90% of the Jews of the United States and Canada, we examine neither entire integrationists nor complete segregationists, but people who want to be Jewish and also participate in the mainstream of American or Canadian life (however the currents in that stream may flow). How they sort out the demands of books that presuppose they are only Jewish, and also only Judaic, defines the problem, and their solutions to the problem form the theory of the matter.

Current social studies of Judaism in America yield a consensus that all surveys have produced.[2] Among the many religious occasions and obligations set forth by the Torah, American Jews in the aggregate do practice some, and do not practice others. Take demography for starters. The United States counts as a "Jewishly identified population" some 6,840,000. Of these, 4.2 million identify themselves as born Jews with the religion, Judaism. They embody all the Judaisms that flourish in North America. Another 1.1 million call themselves born Jews with no religion. Adults of Jewish parentage with some other religion than Judaism are 415,000. Born of Jewish parents, raised as Jewish, and converted to some other religion are 210,000. Jews by choice (converts) are 185,000. Children under 18 being raised in a religion other than Judaism are 700,000 (Kosmin, p. 4). It follows that the "core Jewish population" is 5.5 million, of which approximately 80% (4.4 million) are Jews by religion.

The distinction between the ethnic and the religious—between Jews and Judaists—takes on weight when we examine popular opinion on whether the Jews are a religious group, an ethnic group, a cultural group, or a nationality. Kosmin's report states (p. 28), "Being Jewish as defined by cultural group membership is the clear preference of three of the four identity groups [Jews by birth, religion, Judaism; Jews by choice, converts; Jews by birth with no religion; born and raised Jewish, converted out; adults of Jewish parentage with another current religion]. Definition in terms of ethnic group was the second highest and was cited more frequently than the religious concept by every Jewish identity group." Jews who thought of themselves as a religious group comprised 49% of those who said they were born Jews, religion Judaism; 35% of born Jews with no religion; 56% of born and raised Jews who converted out; and 40% of adults of Jewish parents with another current religion.

The further figure that affects our study—besides the 4.4 million, which defines its parameters—concerns intermarriage patterns. Of all currently married Jews who were born Jewish (1.7 million) 68% are married to someone who was also born Jewish. But, in the language of Kosmin's report, "The choice of marriage partners has changed dramatically over the past few decades. In recent years just over half of born Jews who married, at any age, whether for the first time or not, chose a spouse who was born a Gentile and has remained so, while less than 5% of these marriages include a non-Jewish partner who became a Jew by choice. As a result, since 1985, twice as many mixed couples, that is, born Jew with gentile spouse, have been created as Jewish couples (Jewish with Jewish spouse). This picture ... tends to underestimate the total frequency, because it does not include currently born-Jews divorced or separated from an intermarriage nor Jew-Gentile unmarried couple relationships and living arrangements."

Wertheimer states that "intermarriage has exploded on the American Jewish scene since the mid-1960s, rapidly rising in incident to the point where as many as two out of five Jews who wed marry a partner who was not born Jewish." He points out that 31% of the lay leaders of Reform temples reported having a child with a non-Jewish spouse. Thus, the first thing that captures our attention is that the single most important building block of Judaism, the family—the expression in the here and now of the sacred genealogy of Israel, that is, "the children of Israel," wobbles.

Restricting our attention to the Judaists and the secular Jews (Kosmin's born Jews, religion Judaism and his born Jews with no religion), what do we learn about religious beliefs?

1. The Torah is the actual word of God: 13% of the Judaists concur, and 10% of born Jews with no religion (not a very impressive differential).

2. The Torah is the inspired word of God, but not everything should be taken literally word for word: 38% of the Judaists concur, and 19% of the secularists.

3. The Torah is an ancient book of history and moral precepts recorded by man: 45% of the Judaists, 63% of the secularists.
And 4% of the Judaists and 8% of the secularists had no opinion.

Thus, 13% of the Judaists believe that the Torah is the word of God; another 38% agree that the Torah is the inspired word of God but not literally so; and another 45% value the Torah. If we were to posit that these numbers represent Orthodox, Conservative, and Reform Judaisms, we should not be far off the mark.

In fact, the denominational figures Kosmin's report gives are as follows (current Jewish denominational preferences of adult Jews by religion = our Judaists):

	PROPORTION OF THOSE POLLED	PROPORTION OF HOUSEHOLDS
Orthodox	6.6%	16%
Conservative	37.8%	43%
Reform	42.4%	35%
Reconstructionist	1.4%	2%
Just Jewish	5.4%	

Of the Judaists, 80% are Reform or Conservative, approximately 7% Orthodox. The high level of identification with Orthodoxy is strictly a phenomenon in the greater New York City area. Elsewhere, the percentage of Orthodox Jews in the community of Judaists is still lower (Wertheimer, p. 80). The denominational choice of the rest is scattered. A slightly earlier study by Kosmin (1987) divided the Jews in general as follows: 2% Reconstructionist, 9% Orthodox, 29% Reform, 34% Conservative, and 26% "other" or "just Jewish." It is not clear whether the distinction between Jews and Judaists is reflected in these figures, but the upshot is not in doubt (cf. Wertheimer, pp. 80-81).

Kosmin further observes that there is "a general trend of movement away from traditional Judaism. While one quarter of the born Jewish religion Judaism group was raised in Orthodox households, only 7% report themselves as Orthodox now" (p. 32). Not only so, but "nearly 90% of those now Orthodox were raised as such, thus indicating any movement toward Orthodoxy is relatively small. In contrast to the Orthodox, the Conservative and Reform drew heavily from one or both of the major denominations; one-third of the Conservatives were raised as Orthodox, and one-quarter of the Reform as Conservative, with an additional 12% having been raised Orthodox." Wertheimer also observes that the trend is away from Orthodoxy and from Conservatism as well and toward Reform Judaism: "Nationally, the Conservative movement still commands the allegiance of a plurality of Jews, albeit a shrinking plurality. The main beneficiary of Orthodox and Conservative losses seems to be the Reform movement" (p. 80). As to synagogue affiliation, Kosmin comments, "Synagogue affiliation is the most widespread form of formal Jewish connection, but it characterized only 41% of the entirely Jewish households." He further notes that there is a discrepancy between calling oneself Reform and belonging to a Reform temple: "The distribution of the 860,000 households reporting synagogue membership across the denominations shows that the Reform plurality, which was evidence in denominational preferences, does not translate directly into affiliation. By contrast, the Orthodox are more successful in affiliating their potential constituency."

What about religious practice of the Judaists—the center of concern for this inquiry? Here the figures cover only three matters:

fast on the Day of Atonement	61%
attend synagogue on High Holy Days	59%
attend synagogue weekly	11%

Studies over the past several decades have replicated these results: many people go to Passover seders, a great many also observe the so-called High Holy Days (in the Torah, "the days of awe," that is, Rosh Hashanah, the New Year, and Yom Kippur, the Day of Atonement). So we may ask, why do approximately half of the Judaists who worship in community at all do so only three days a year? How do they know what is fit and proper? Why this day, not that?

As to rites at home and household practices, Kosmin shifts to entirely Jewish households, as against mixed Jewish and gentile households, that is, from the Judaist to the Jewish (and a sensible shift at that):

attend Passover seder	86%
never have a Christmas tree	82%
light Hanukkah candles	77%
light Sabbath candles	44%
belong to a synagogue	41%
eat kosher meat all the time	17%

What makes Passover different from all other holidays? What makes

Sabbath candles (all the more so, the weekly Sabbath as a holy day of rest) only half as important as Hanukkah candles (one week out of the year)?

Since the Torah devotes considerable attention to the foods that may sustain the life of holy Israel, and since the ethnic Jews too identify foods as particularly Jewish, we may ask about the matter of observance of dietary rules in Conservative Judaism, which affirms them and regards them as a key indicator of piety. Charles S. Liebman and Saul Shapiro report that among the Conservative Jews they surveyed, 5% of the men and 6.4% of the women claim to observe dietary laws both at home and away (by the standards of Conservative Judaism, which are somewhat more lenient then those of Orthodoxy).[3] And 29.2% of the men and 28.8% of the women have kosher homes but do not keep the dietary taboos away from home. Thus, approximately a third of the Conservative homes appear to be conducted in accordance with the laws of kosher food. Liebman and Shapiro point out that the home of the parents in this group was also kosher, and observance of the dietary laws correlates with Jewish education: "Of the children receiving a day school education, 66% come from kosher homes; of all those who attended Camp Ramah [a Jewish education summer camp run by the Conservative movement], 53% came from kosher homes; this despite the fact that only 34% of the parents report their homes are kosher. The differences are even more dramatic if one bears in mind that a disproportionate number of older Conservative synagogue members have kosher homes, which means that their children were educated at a time when day school education was much less widespread in the Jewish community."

Along these same lines Steven M. Cohen introduces the metaphor of "an artichoke syndrome," where, he says, "the outer layers of the most traditional forms of Jewish expression are peeled away until only the most essential and minimal core of involvement remains, and then that also succumbs to the forces of assimilation. . . . According to assimilationist expectations, ritual observance and other indicators of Jewish involvement decline successively from parents to children."[4] But current studies do not "support a theory predicting uniform decline in ritual practice from one generation to the next. Rather, it suggests intergenerational flux with a limited movement toward a low level of observance entailing Passover seder attendance, Hanukkah candle lighting, and fasting on Yom Kippur."[5] In other studies, Steven M. Cohen speaks of "moderately affiliated Jews," who nearly unanimously "celebrate High Holidays, Hanukkah and Passover, belong to synagogues when their children approach age 12 and 13, send their children to afternoon school or Sunday school, and at least occasionally support the Federation [=UJA] campaigns."[6] Cohen speaks of "broad affection for Jewish family, food, and festivals." Here, Cohen's report provides especially valuable data. He explains "why Jews feel so affectionate toward their holidays":

> One theme common to the six items [celebrated by from 70 to over 90% surveyed] is family. Holidays are meaningful because they connect Jews with their family-related memories, experiences, and aspirations. Respondents say that they want to be with their families on Jewish holidays, that they recall fond childhood memories at those times, and that they especially want to connect their own children with Jewish traditions at holiday time. Moreover, holidays evoke a certain transcendent significance; they have ethnic and religious import; they connect one with the history of the Jewish people, and they bear a meaningful religious message. Last, food . . . constitutes a major element in Jews' affection for the holidays.[7]

The holidays that are most widely celebrated in this report remain the same as in the others: Passover, Hanukkah, and the High Holy Days. By contrast, "relatively few respondents highly value three activities: observing the Sabbath, adult Jewish education, and keeping kosher." The question comes to the fore once again: why those rites and not others?

Concerning Israeli matters, among the Judaists, 31% have visited the state of Israel, 35% have close family or friends living there; among the ethnic Jews (not Judaists), the figures are 11% and 20%. What makes the state of Israel so important to the Judaists?

As for charity, including Israel-centered charity, UJA for instance (once more speaking of entirely Jewish households):

contributed to a Jewish charity in 1989	62%
contributed to UJA/Federation campaign in 1989	45%
celebrate Israeli Independence Day	18%

And, for comparison:

contributed to a secular charity in 1989   67%

contributed to a political campaign in 1988–
1990   36%

Commenting on the Kosmin report, Ari L. Goldman stated, "In a radical change from just a generation ago, American Jews today are as likely to marry non-Jews as Jews. But even as this assimilation accelerates, Jews are clinging to religious traditions. . . . These trends—one away from tradition, the other maintaining tradition—are spelled out." (*New York Times*, Friday, June 7, 1991)

Covering a variety of issues, Jack Wertheimer proposes to "evaluate the state of contemporary Jewish religious life" (Wertheimer, p. 63), with special attention to changing patterns of religious observance, which concern this inquiry into the contrast between book Judaism and practiced Judaism. Orthodoxy, conceded by all parties to be closest in popular observance to the Judaism described in the holy books, retains its young people, but at the same time loses its older population—a disproportionately large component of its numbers—to death, with from two to three times as many Orthodox Jews over age 65 as between 18 and 45; so the gap between the Judaism of the books as lived by everyday Jews and the conduct of the generality of Jews is in fact growing wider. Synagogue attendance rates vary, but generally decline. According to Wertheimer, in the early 1980s approximately 44% of Americans claimed they attended services weekly, and 24% of American Jews did. That figure is high. "In most communities between one third and one-half of all Jews attend religious services either never or only on the High Holy Days" (Wertheimer, p. 85).

Dividing the country by communities yields various statistics on diverse religious practices. For the sake of simplifying the picture (for the variations are not formidable) we shall review Wertheimer's "practice of selected observances, by community" (pp. 88ff.):

	New York	Philadelphia	St. Louis	Phoenix	Rochester
attends seder	89%	89%	71%	81%	80%
lights Hanukkah candles	76%	78%	80%	78%	78%

has mezuzah	70%	71%	76%	57%	NA
fasts on Yom Kippur	67%	67%	NA	NA	63%
lights Sabbath candles	37%	32%	28%	NA	33%
buys only kosher meat	36%	NA	19%	NA	NA
uses two sets of dishes, meat and dairy	30%	16%	15%	9%	23%
handles no money on the Sabbath	12%	NA	NA	4%	NA
refrains from transport on the Sabbath	NA	5%	5%	4%	NA
has Christmas tree (sometimes or frequently)	NA	NA	14%	NA	15%

These figures show a fair amount of variation but overall confirm the results of the Kosmin study. Some religious practices are widespread, others are not. Moreover, if we distinguish, as Kosmin does, between those who say they are Jews by religion and those who say they are not, the probability that the percentages of Judaists who practice the rites listed here is probably higher than indicated.

The available figures rarely tell us about other rites, for instance, what percentage of Jews who marry other Jews and who also identify as Judaists marry in a Judaic rite, and what percentage do not? Neither do they reveal what percentage of Jews circumcise their sons, whether they do so eight days after birth, whether it is done by a ritual circumciser (mohel), or a doctor. Here we have some intriguing data. Cohen notes[8] that "a large proportion, 55%, of respondents say it is extremely important that their children have sons ritually circumcised; another 18% say it is very important. These proportions far exceed those on marrying another Jew—33% say marrying another Jew is extremely important for their children, as opposed to the 55% for circumcising their grandsons." The upshot is somewhat curious: grandparents are more concerned that their grandsons be circumcised than that their sons marry

Jewish women. Since the child of a gentile woman is, in the law of Judaism, a Gentile, it turns out that these grandparents favor the circumcision of (specified) Gentiles as part of what "a good Jew" wants. We shall return to that anomaly in due course.

What percentage of Jews are buried by a rabbi and buried in a Jewish cemetery? What percentage of Judaists have Judaic last rites? For these and similar questions we rely on guesswork, but the general impression is that most Jews who marry other Jews have a religious ceremony; most Judaists are buried with Judaic rites; the rite of circumcision, among Reform Jews, tends to be transformed into a merely surgical procedure but the rite is exceedingly common among American Jews. These and other impressions do not have the same authority as the results of the surveys. They suffice to suggest that Judaists practice rites of passage—circumcision or some other rite at the birth of a child (synagogue service for naming sons and daughters, for instance); bar or bat mitzvah; marriage by a rabbi and a cantor under a Judaic marriage canopy; burial. Add to this very high levels of observance of Passover, Hanukkah, and other home rites, and we form the impression of a religion that enjoys substantial everyday observance of rites that involve the family and the home.

But it would be a considerable error to ignore certain broadly practiced activities that characterize Jews in America and that form a major public component of their community, for instance, philanthropic and political activities, which are frequently explained within the framework of Judaism. So there is a public and communal Judaism, as much as a Judaism for home and family, and that too demands description and explanation.

If, then, we wish to describe the large center of American Jews, those who are both ethnically Jewish and religiously Judaic—estimated by Steven M. Cohen to number about half of the American Jews—we may do so in the terms Cohen has provided. He gives these generalizations that pertain to our problem:[9]

> The moderately affiliated are proud of their identity as Jews, of Jews generally, and of Judaism.
> They combine universalist and particularist impulses; they are ambivalent about giving public expression to their genuinely felt attachment to things Jewish.

They are especially fond of the widely celebrated Jewish holidays as well as the family experiences and special foods that are associated with them.

They celebrate High Holidays, Hanukkah and Passover as well as most major American civic holidays . . . .

They vest importance in those Jewish activities they perform; and they regard those activities they fail to undertake as of little import. Accordingly, they are happy with themselves as Jews; they believe they are "good Jews."

Their primary Jewish goal for their children is for them to maintain Jewish family continuity . . . .

The Holocaust and anti-Semitism are among the most powerful Jewish symbols . . . .

The moderately affiliated believe God exists, but they have little faith in an active and personal God.

They are voluntarists, they affirm a right to select those Jewish customs they regard as personally meaningful, and unlike many intensive Jews, most of the moderately affiliated reject the obligatory nature of halakhah [laws, norms].

They endorse broad, abstract principles of Jewish life (such as knowing the fundamentals of Judaism) but fail to support narrower, more concrete normative demands (such as regular text study or sending their children to Jewish day schools).

The moderately affiliated prefer in-marriage but fail to oppose out-marriage with a great sense of urgency.

They support [the state of] Israel, but only as a subordinate concern, one lacking any significant influence on the private sphere of Jewish practice.

To the moderately affiliated, "good Jews" are those who affiliate with other Jews and Jewish institutions.

This description fits a large segment of Judaists, who in some ways conform, and in other ways do not conform, to book Judaism. Their religion presents us with a problem of interpretation: How do these people know the difference between what matters and what does not— not only Passover as against Pentecost (Shavuot); but circumcision as against intermarriage; the Holocaust and anti-Semitism as against the state of Israel; the existence of God as against God's active caring? The key lies in Cohen's statement, "they affirm a right to select."

In a world governed by rationality, reasonable explanations guide people in the choices they make. Ideas matter; learning and reasoning count; people make rational decisions based on what they know and a thoughtful response to the problems they wish to solve. What people know—that is, the problems facing them—these form the social order in which they find themselves. In the interplay of ideas and the social order I locate what to me makes sense—common sense, self-evidence. Now I cannot demonstrate that people's ideas stand independent of other components of their consciousness, their emotions for instance; nor can I show that ideas enjoy an independent stance, as against rationalizations of some condition of an other-than-intellectual character. I can only offer what strikes me as a plausible way of reading what people say and do.

And that leads me to the question that occupies us to the end of this book: What defines the interplay between the theology of various Judaic rites and the practice of those rites at large? The answer, as I shall demonstrate, lies in the interplay between the meaning of rites and the social situation of the faithful. When we know what a rite has to say and to whom it is supposed to speak, we may frame a theory of why this, not that. To spell out that theory I now set forth some of the main observances and activities of Judaism, in both intellectual (theological) and social context: what Judaism says, to whom it means to speak, who hears and responds. At Sinai it was "we shall do and we shall hear" (= obey). Here, it is, "we shall hear and we may or may not do." The important question is, What is heard and by whom?

PART II

WHY THIS?

CHAPTER 3

What the People Do in Synagogue

The Day of Atonement and Worship in the Synagogue on the High Holy Days

◇

On some occasions large numbers of people come to the synagogue; on others, of equal sanctity in the theology of Judaism, they do not. They come on Passover but not Pentecost or Tabernacles. Why? Circumcision of some kind (if not in full accord with the requirement of the law of Judaism) is common but not ritual immersion when a woman's menstrual period has ended. Why this, not that? The answer is simple: the sanctifying rites engage and enchant when done at home or at life's turnings. Rites bearing the same message and originating in the same way gain no entry for the mass of Judaists when they require communal and collective action. Other rites, appealing to other myths (as I shall explain later on), by contrast do win the credence of these same Judaists. We begin with a general theory of matters, then test our theory against the specific practices of real people living ordinary lives.

The general theory is a simple one: in America, religion is personal and private, familial rather than communal. That explains the observance of Passover, which is a home rite, but not Pentecost, which finds its observance principally in the synagogue. Passover bears a message Jews hear—"the season of our freedom"—while Tabernacles, also celebrated at home with outdoor meals in a decorated bower, does not.

The message of Tabernacles—"the season of our rejoicing"—somehow finds no hearing for the vast majority of Judaists. For them, it appears, Judaism forms an expression of assertion in the face of a denying

world, not a moment of sheer human pleasure and thanks in response
to a beneficent one. Judaism then bears a plausible message of resentment
and affirmation despite the other side; but its many more messages of
joy and sheer enjoyment fall on deaf ears.

Why this, not that, when it comes to personal rites or rites of passage?
Why circumcision but not immersion in a ritual immersion pool (*miqveh*)
when a woman completes her menstrual cycle each month? The one
is a rite of passage, the other, a rite of a different passage. Rites of
passage pertain, rites celebrated in the context of the household transform—especially if they contain the message people find authentic to
their human situation. But a deep intrusion is involved in the regulation
of sexual activity between husband and wife. That (the Judaists in general
concur) seems a bit much—self-evidently.

To be sure, within Jewry, and especially for Judaists (who are also
Jews, as ethnic as the rest), there are also public and communal occasions.
Being Jewish is public and political; Jews are Jews together and for
shared purposes, not only at home for private ones. So public community
celebrations do occur. But these derive from a different myth from that
of the Judaism of Scripture and tradition. When Jews come together
for public and communal action, they have a different story to tell
themselves than the story about the "Israel" they form, in direct succession to ancient Israel. Why? All of the rites that attract broad public
support involve either the private person (the High Holy Days, rites of
passage) or center upon the home (Passover and Hanukkah); they all
bear a plausible, self-evidently valid message about Israel in Egypt,
which is to say, the Jews in North America.

North American Jews identify as their own rites that are personal
and familial, choosing from the menu made available by the Judaism
of the dual Torah only those occasions that can be celebrated at home,
on the one side, or celebrating rites of passage, on the other. What is
public and communal in the received Judaism of Scripture and tradition
is neglected; what is private and personal is immensely popular.

That does not mean Jews in North America live out their Judaisms
off the public stage. They have not privatized their Judaic life. They
have treated as personal and private only part of it, the part that they
find pertinent in the received tradition. What that does mean is that
another Judaism than the received one is going to present its myth to

compete with the received one. Its rites will compete with those familiar from tradition. Jews reject received religious rites that involve them in public and communal religious celebrations; for the purpose of public life, they derive their myths and rites elsewhere. While religion has become private, personal, and familial, there is another aspect of Jews' collective life, a political one, that draws them out of home and family and invokes a different, and a public, human experience of being Jewish. So there are parallel Judaisms, the one for home and family, the other for community and the Judaic social order. They coincide and intersect, but they are not the same thing and are readily distinguished from each other.

That general theory of why Jews do one thing and not another is challenged every September by the advent of the New Year (Rosh Hashanah) and Day of Atonement (Yom Kippur). These are the two seasons of public and communal Judaism practiced by most Judaists. Two-thirds of all Judaists say they fast on Yom Kippur, and it goes without saying, they spend most of that day in prayer. Yom Kippur forms the climax of the penitential season, which for Judaists in the United States and Canada starts with the New Year. In book Judaism and in the practiced Judaism of Orthodoxy, the season commences a month earlier, with the lunar month of Elul (generally, mid-August), when the ram's horn (*shofar*) is sounded in synagogue services just as it is on the New Year, and when the same Penitential Psalms are added to the liturgy that American Judaism has selected for its "high holy days." Why do people attend the synagogue worship on the most intensely spiritual of all occasions, but not on the intervening Sabbath or on any other? Why this, not that?

For their uncompromising, sheer spirituality, these days evoke the most profound religious emotions. The synagogue takes the form of a gathering of the saints, with much introspection, confession of sin, quest for inner purity. For a few hours, we might as well find ourselves in a medieval cloister or yeshiva, where people live in the here and now solely in preparation for the life to come, and really believe in sin and punishment, but also in repentance and forgiveness.

The prevailing view that Americans in general do not believe in sin and divine retribution makes surprising the mass concurrence on these particular days as centerpieces of the faith. Synagogues, sparsely attended on Sabbaths and festivals, are crowded on the Days of Awe. And that fact presents a puzzle. Clearly, Judaism does work its enchantment and transforms some moments, but not others. Since there are plenty of empty seats on the Sabbath between the New Year and the Day of Atonement, as on all other Sabbaths, it is not the season alone, any more than baseball teams without a shot at the pennant can fill a stadium in August. The point is that the same Judaism, invoking the same symbolic system and mythic structure, in some instances transforms but in others changes nothing. If people respond to one rite and not another, we ask what makes one rite compelling, another irrelevant. Why do two-thirds of all Judaists come to synagogue on Thursday and Friday, the New Year, but Saturday following, which is the Sabbath, perhaps 10% may find their way to the same seats?

First, let us listen with some care to the answers of the Days of Awe, for through these we shall find it possible to state the questions, from which, in our further step outward, we shall reach that larger social context that frames the whole. Rosh Hashanah and Yom Kippur together mark days of solemn penitence at the start of the autumn festival season. The words of the liturgy create a world of personal introspection, individual judgment. The turning of the year marks a time of looking backward. It is melancholy, like the falling leaves, but hopeful, as with the above example of teams out of the pennant race: next year is another season.

The answer of the Days of Awe concerns life and death, which take mythic form in affirmations of God's rule and judgment. The words create a world aborning, the old now gone, the new just now arriving. The New Year, Rosh Hashanah, celebrates the creation of the world: "Today the world was born." The time of new beginnings also marks endings: "On the New Year the decree is issued: Who will live and who will die?" At the New Year—so the words state—humanity is inscribed for life or death in the heavenly books for the coming year, and on the Day of Atonement the books are sealed. The world comes out to hear these words. The season is rich in celebration. The synagogues on that day are filled—whether with penitents or people who merely wish to be there hardly matters. The New Year is a day of remembrance on which the deeds of all creatures are reviewed. The principal themes of the words invoke creation and God's rule over creation; revelation and God's rule in the Torah for the created world; and redemption— God's ultimate plan for the world.

On the birthday of the world God made, God asserts his sovereignty, as in the New Year Prayer:

> Our God and God of our Fathers, rule over the whole world in Your honor ... and appear in Your glorious might to all those who dwell in the civilization of Your world, so that everything made will know that You made it, and every creature discern that You have created him, so that all in whose nostrils is breath may say, "The Lord, the God of Israel is king, and His kingdom extends over all."[1]

Liturgical words concerning divine sovereignty, divine memory, and divine disclosure correspond to creation, revelation, and redemption. Sovereignty is established by creation of the world. Judgment depends upon law: "From the beginning You made this, Your purpose known...." And therefore, since people have been told what God requires of them, they are judged:

> On this day sentence is passed upon countries, which to the sword and which to peace, which to famine and which to plenty, and each creature is judged today for life or death. Who is not judged on this day? For the remembrance of every creature comes before You, each man's deeds and destiny, words and way....

These are strong words for people to hear. As life unfolds and people grow reflective, the Days of Awe seize the imagination: I live, I die, sooner or later it comes to all. The call for inner contemplation implicit in the mythic words elicits deep response.

The theme of revelation is further combined with redemption; the ram's horn, or *shofar,* which is sounded in the synagogue during daily worship for a month before the Rosh Hashanah festival, serves to unite the two:

> You did reveal Yourself in a cloud of glory.... Out of heaven You made them [Israel] hear Your voice.... Amid thunder and lightning You revealed Yourself to them, and while the *shofar* sounded You shined forth upon them.... Our God and God of our fathers, sound the great *shofar* for our freedom. Lift up the ensign to gather our exiles.... Lead us happily to Zion Your city, Jerusalem the place of Your sanctuary.

The complex themes of the New Year, the most "theological" of Jewish holy occasions, thus weave together the tapestry of a highly charged moment in a world subject to the personal scrutiny of a most active God.

What of the Day of Atonement? Here too we hear the same answers, see the unfolding of a single process of transformation of secular into sacred time. Yom Kippur is the most personal, solemn, and moving of the Days of Awe. It is the Sabbath of Sabbaths and it is marked by fasting and continuous prayer. On it, the Jew makes confession:

> Our God and God of our fathers, may our prayer come before You. Do not hide Yourself from our supplication, for we are not so arrogant or stiff-necked as to say before You ... "We are righteous and have not sinned." But we have sinned.
>
> We are guilt laden, we have been faithless, we have robbed. . . .
>
> We have committed iniquity, caused unrighteousness, have been presumptuous . . . .
>
> We have counseled evil, scoffed, revolted, blasphemed.

The Hebrew confession is built upon an alphabetical acrostic, as if by making certain every letter is represented, God, who knows human secrets, will combine them into appropriate words. The very alphabet bears witness against us before God. Then:

> What shall we say before You who dwell on high? What shall we tell You who live in heaven? Do You not know all things, both the hidden and the revealed? You know the secrets of eternity, the most hidden mysteries of life. You search the innermost recesses, testing men's feelings and heart. Nothing is concealed from You or hidden from Your eyes. May it therefore be Your will to forgive us our sins, to pardon us for our iniquities, to grant remission for our transgressions.

A further list of sins follows, built on alphabetical lines. Prayers to be spoken by the congregation are all in the plural: "For the sin which we have sinned against You with the utterance of the lips. . . . For the sin which we have sinned before You openly and secretly." The community takes upon itself responsibility for what is done. All Israel is part of one community, one body, and all are responsible for the acts of each. The sins confessed are mostly against society, against one's fellowmen; few pertain to ritual laws. At the end comes a final word:

> O my God, before I was formed, I was nothing. Now that I have been formed, it is as though I had not been formed, for I am dust in my life, more so after death. Behold I am before You like a vessel filled with shame and confusion. May it be Your will ... that I may no more sin, and forgive the sins I have already committed in Your abundant compassion.

While much of the liturgy speaks of "we," the individual focus dominates, beginning to end. The words say "we" but mean me. The Days of Awe speak to the heart of the individual, telling a story of judgment and atonement. So the individual Jew stands before God possessing no merits, yet hopeful of God's love and compassion. If that is the answer, can there be any doubt about the question? I think not. The power of the Days of Awe derives from the sentiments and emotions aroused by the theme of those days: what is happening to me? Where am I going?

Moments of introspection and reflection serve as guideposts in people's lives. That is why people treasure such moments and respond to the opportunities that define them. The themes of the Days of Awe stated in mythic terms address the human condition, and the message penetrates to the core of human concerns about life and death, the year past, the year beyond, the wrongs and the sins and the remissions and atonement. Viewed in context, the Days of Awe replay the music we hear on Sabbath and festival, at Passover and under the marriage canopy, at the circumcision and at the grace after meals. No occasion within the liturgical life omits sanctification, none forgets salvation; none fails to speak of sanctification and salvation in the language of Torah and God's rule. A review of the range of public and communal celebration shows how profoundly integrated are the individual and the community, the private and the public blending into a single pattern of this-worldly sanctification aimed at salvation at the end of time.

A religion says the same thing over and over again, in many different ways repeating a single and singular message. In fact, like a fugue, the Judaic way of life joins into one harmony three distinct voices, three separate cycles, one voice in the rhythm of the year, the second voice in the rhythm of the week, the third voice in the rhythm of a person's life. A bird's-eye view of the whole will provide a vision that, in a

Orthodox Jews inspect the quality of the *lulav*
(myrtle and willow) to be waved on each of the
first seven days of Sukkot.

moment, will allow the reader to discern why this, not that; why some
things work their wonder and others do not.

The polyphonal Judaic year follows the lunar calendar, so the appearance of the new moon marks the beginning of a month, and that
is celebrated. There are two critical moments in the unfolding of the
year, the first full moon after the autumnal equinox, and the first full
moon after the vernal equinox. These mark the time of heightened
celebration. To understand how the rhythm of the year unfolds, however,
we begin with the new moon of the month of Tishri, corresponding
to September. That marks the New Year, Rosh Hashanah. Ten days
later comes Yom Kippur, which commemorates the rite described in
Leviticus 16, and marks God's judgment and forgiveness of humanity.
Five days afterward is the full moon, which is the beginning of the

festival of Tabernacles—Sukkot. That festival lasts for eight days and ends with a day of solemn assembly, *Shemini Aseret*, and of rejoicing of the Torah, *Simhat Torah.*

Thus, according to the books, nearly the whole month of Tishri is spent in celebration: eating, drinking, praying, studying, enjoying and celebrating God's sovereignty, creation, revelation, redemption, as the themes of the festivals and solemn celebrations of the season work themselves out. The next major sequence of celebration follows the first new moon after the vernal equinox, which begins the month of Nisan and culminates, at its full moon, with Passover—Pesah—which commemorates the Exodus of Israel from Egypt and celebrates Israel's freedom, bestowed by God. Fifty days thereafter comes the festival of Pentecost—Shavuot— which commemorates the giving of the Torah at Mount Sinai. Other occasions for celebration exist, but the New Year, the Day of Atonement, Tabernacles, Passover, and Pentecost are the main holy days.

Just as the Days of Awe—the New Year and the Day of Atonement— and the festivals of Tabernacles, Passover, and Pentecost mark the passage of the lunar year, so the Sabbath marks the movement of time through the week. The sanctification of the Sabbath, observed on the seventh day, Saturday, is one of the Ten Commandments. It is the single happiest moment in Judaism, and, coming as it does every week, the Sabbath sheds its light on the everyday. On the Sabbath people do no servile labor, and they devote themselves to sacred activities, including both synagogue worship and study of the Torah, as well as to eating, drinking, relaxing, and enjoying themselves. The song for the Sabbath day, Psalm 92, expresses the spirit of this observance: *"It is good to give thanks to the Lord."* Faithful Jews find in the Sabbath the meaning of their everyday lives.

According to the same books, the passage of the individual's life, from birth to death, marks out the third of the three cycles, the three joined voices, the cycles that convey the spirit of the Torah. The principal points are birth, puberty, marriage, and death. Birth in the case of males is marked by circumcision on the eighth day. Nowadays in the synagogue the birth of both sons and daughters is celebrated by a rite of naming of the child. The celebration of a child's becoming responsible to carry out the religious duties that are called *mitzvot*, or commandments, entering the status known as *bar mitzvah* for the boy and *bat mitzvah* for the girl, takes place in the synagogue in a simple way. The young

Two Reform rabbis conduct a naming ceremony for a
newborn Jewish girl.

man or woman is called to read the Torah, and the prophetic passage
of the day is also read by the newly responsible young adult. We have
already noted the marriage ceremony. Rites of death, as we shall see in
chapter 5, involve a clear recognition that God rules and is the true
and just authority over all humanity. The memorial prayer, or *Qaddish*
for mourners, expresses the worshiper's recognition of God's holiness
and dominion and states the hope for the coming of the Messiah. In a
few words these events of celebration, which one might call "life-style
events," define life under the law and explain how Judaists seek to live
in accord with God's will, which is that Israel live the holy life in the
here and now and await salvation at the end of time.

That raises the question with great force: why within an integrated and coherent system such as I have described do people celebrate one thing and not another? The books present music with rhythm, harmony, coherence, melody. The people take a piece of the rhythm from one place, a snatch of the melody from some other, a snippet of the harmony used here, and bellow out the whole as their hymn to God. (And, I hasten to add, God's hearing is better than ours: to God it's music too.) So the issue is not belief or nonbelief. People who can believe that they are really slaves redeemed from Pharaoh in Egypt, for whom (as we shall see) the pretense that they are Adam and Eve in Eden resonates, who are willing to have their son's foreskin cut off on the eighth day after birth—such people will believe and do anything. There is nothing more or less compelling in the reason for the Sabbath than the reason for the Passover banquet rite, although, considering the values embedded in the Sabbath, that rite enjoys a more direct relevance to this country and this time than does Passover. If the issue is not that the more reasonable is the more practiced, then what explains the power of some words and not others? In my view, the issue is the question and the answer—people will believe all sorts of things and yet deny the end of their nose if they want to.

In chapter 7 we shall review the neglected rites of the synagogue— those of daily worship, Sabbaths, and festivals. As we shall see, the three historical-agricultural festivals—Pesah, Sukkot, and Shavuot—pertain, in varying ways and combinations, to the themes we have already considered in this chapter. Pesah is the festival of redemption and points toward the Torah revelation of the Shavuot. The harvest festival in the autumn celebrates not only creation, but especially redemption. Like the Sabbath, these festivals take ordinary people and turn them into Israel; they take profane time and sanctify it. The same reason that accounts for the neglect of the Sabbath explains the limited popularity of Sukkot, Shavuot, and the observance of Passover. But at stake in holy time is holiness, the transformation of a world by reason of an occasion, and if God took account of numbers, what would he make of Israel? In the comparison of size as of space, no magic works. But to change life—that is true enchantment. The Sabbath and its counterpart festivals transform life through the reordering of time and space, the reconciliation of action and community at rest. The reason why not, as I shall explain in chapter 7, is contained in the uncompromisingly public character of the Sabbath and the festivals. They are occasions of community, events of civilization. They vastly transcend home and family, though for those who keep them, they define home and family. It is not that they ask too much. It is that what they ask is not found urgent or even relevant to people living private lives.

What the People
Do at Home
The Passover Seder and Hanukkah

◇

The vast majority of American Jews take note of Passover and attend
a Passover seder, that is, a meal in a home with a family—or a family
invented for the occasion. A sizable proportion of the community also
kindles Hanukkah lights. The two important aspects of Passover are
the fact that it is a home celebration and the message of the occasion
strikes home. Here is a perfect match between the social setting and
the statement that the faith makes for that occasion. My argument is
that Passover and Hanukkah enjoy vast popularity because they speak
to Jews where they hear the Judaic message—at home and with their
families. Their message (and it is one message) strikes home because it
matches the sense of how things are in the social order of America and
Canada as Jews perceive it. Passover is one of the rites of home and
family, and the message of the occasion, to the family, fits the Jews'
sense of what they are and how they live.

◇

Passover

How does the message match the contemporary moment that North
American Jews define for themselves? The Passover seder is a home

63

Participants in the Passover seder meal sing blessings and prayers
before the start of the meal.

banquet rite, observed on the first night (for Reformed) and the first
and second nights (for Conservative and Orthodox Jews) of the festival
that commemorates the liberation of Israel from Egypt. It is called in
the liturgy "the season of our freedom." The meal consumed with
ceremony turns people into something other than what they think they
are and puts them down square into the path of an onrushing history.
In the presence of symbols both visual and verbal, in the formation of
family and friends into an Israel redeemed from Egypt, people become
something else, and words work that wonder. This is a rite of transformation, and, I maintain, when we understand the message of the
occasion, we shall grasp why North American Jews have made it their
own, as they clearly have.

At the festival of Passover, which coincides with the first full moon
after the vernal equinox, Jewish families gather around their tables for
a holy meal. There they retell the story of the Exodus from Egypt.
With unleavened bread and sanctified wine, they celebrate the liberation
of slaves from Pharaoh's bondage. There is, at the rite, a single formula
that captures the moment and causes us to understand how the "we"
of the family becomes the "we" of Israel, and how the eternal and
perpetual coming of spring is made to mark a singular moment, a one-
time act on the stage in the unfolding of linear time:

For ever after, in every generation, *every Israelite must think of himself or herself as having gone forth from Egypt* (emphasis added).[1]

This is a curious passage indeed. It is one thing to tell Jews to think of themselves in one way, rather than in some other. It is quite a different thing to explain why Jews respond to the demand—and they do respond.

Jews find the rite critical because they make history their own, allowing what happened long ago to tell them who they are this minute. What is it that makes credible the statement, "*We* went forth . . ." and why do people sit down for supper and announce, "It was not only our forefathers that the Holy One, blessed be He, redeemed; *us too, the living*, He redeemed together with them"? I cannot imagine a less plausible statement, a more compelling invitation to derision. "We" were not there. Pharaoh has been dead for quite some time. Egypt languishes in the rubbish heap of history. North American Jews are nobody's slaves, so wherein the enchantment? The "we" of family is told it is someone else, in another time and another place. And that, I think, can take place only because the family and friends now assembled in mind and imagination have already transformed themselves. Then they can be told to change and be instructed on their roles. If we review the provocative themes of the script for the drama, we may pick out those components of the everyday that are subjected to transformation. In simpler language, we can identify in the message of the occasion the meaning that people find so congruent with the world as they perceive it.

One theme stands out: we, here and now, are really living then and there. So for example:

We were slaves of Pharaoh in Egypt and the Lord our God brought us forth from there with a mighty hand and an outstretched arm. And if the Holy One, blessed be He, had not brought our fathers forth from Egypt, then we and our descendants would still be slaves to Pharaoh in Egypt. And so, even if all of us were full of wisdom, understanding, sages and well informed in the Torah, we should still be obligated to repeat again the story of the Exodus from Egypt; and whoever treats as an important matter the story of the Exodus from Egypt is praiseworthy.

And again:

This is the bread of affliction which our ancestors ate in the land of Egypt. Let all who are hungry come and eat with us, let all who are needy come and celebrate the Passover with us This year here, next year in the land of Israel; this year slave, next year free people.

And yet a third statement:

This is the promise which has stood by our forefathers and stands by us. For neither once, nor twice, nor three times was our destruction planned; in every generation they rise against us, and in every generation God delivers us from their hands into freedom, out of anguish into joy, out of mourning into festivity, out of darkness into light, out of bondage into redemption.

Religion is never subtle and always forceful. It states only a few simple messages, and it says them in every possible medium. As though the implicit premise were not clear, let us revert to the point at which we began and hear how it is stated in so many words:

For ever after, in every generation, *every Israelite must think of himself or herself as having gone forth from Egypt* [emphasis added]. For we read in the Torah: "In that day thou shalt teach thy son, saying: All this is because of what God did for me when I went forth from Egypt." It was not only our forefathers that the Holy One, blessed be He, redeemed; us too, the living, He redeemed together with them, as we learn from the verse in the Torah: "And He brought us out from thence, so that He might bring us home, and give us the land which he pledged to our forefathers."

If we ask, therefore, what experience in the here and now is taken up and transformed by enchantment into the then and the there, we move from the rite to the reality. That progress tells us what troubles these people and makes playacting plausible as they turn their lives into metaphor, themselves into actors, the everyday into pretense and drama.

And this brings us back to our issue: why Passover but not either of the other two principal festivals of Judaism—Shavuot or Sukkot? The question takes on urgency when we remind ourselves that we confront the single most popular and widely observed rite of Judaism. What speaks so ubiquitously, with such power, that pretty much everybody who wants in joins in? In my view, the message penetrates to the heart of people who remember the murder of six million Jews in the near past, and who know that in the present they too are a minority and at risk, if not in politics, then in psychology.

Jews are not slaves in North America, but the freest and most fortunate generation of Jews of all time. So if everything is right, why is the one rite that requires people to remember misery the one they find self-evidently critical to their religious system? What troubles Jews in a free society is not that they are not free, but that they are uncomfortable with the kind of freedom that makes them what they are: free to be different. At important turnings in their lives, people do not want to be different, especially if the difference bears (some) negative burdens.

Now it is a fact that Jews do experience anti-Semitism—not the violent, racist kind that ultimately led to the murder of most of the Jews in continental Europe in World War II, but still, dislike for being unlike. But, in general, Jews do not live in an anti-Semitic society, any more than blacks live in a racist society. Goodwill outweighs bigotry, and, besides, in the ways that count, racism and bigotry violate the law. North American society can do little that it has not already done to give a secure and welcoming place to everyone, but the one thing the United States cannot offer the Jews is a Jewish nation. Everyone is a minority somehow, and few identify themselves as part of the majority, whether as to race or religion or in any of the other variables and distinctions that people identify with significant difference.

And who wants to be different? What match do I claim to find, then, between the occasion and its message? This home rite speaks with great power, in a way in which other home rites do not, because the rite transforms what people feel into a sentiment they can recognize; they become a simile for something more—and more noble—than what they feel. In theoretical language, Jews in North America drawn to their dinner parties enter an anguish drawn from mythic being because that anguish imparts to their ordinary life that metaphoric quality— that status as simile—that makes sense of the already perceived.

The Jews are a minority, small in numbers, compensating in visibility. So far as they differ from "the others," Jews fantasize that there is a majority that is alike in all respects because everyone who is not Jewish is the same, that is, is (merely) gentile. In meeting this imagined world out there, Jews confront not a critical but a chronic discomfort. To be different—whatever the difference—requires explanation; it provokes resentment; it creates tension demanding resolution and pain requiring remission. For the young, difference is deadly. For the middle-aged, difference demands explanation and compensation, and it may well exact the cost of diminished opportunity. For the individual may not be different from other individuals, but families always do retain that mark of difference from other families, and that in the very nature of their existence. Passover celebrates the family of Israel and is celebrated by the families of Israel. So Passover, with its rhetoric of rejoicing for freedom, plays out in a minor key the song of liberation: today slaves, next year free, today here, next year in "Jerusalem" (that is, not the real Jerusalem but the imagined, heavenly one). That is why, when they read, "We see ourselves as if . . . ," they do not burst out laughing and call for the main course.

When people tell themselves that they too were slaves but have been freed, the words invoke the metaphor of the Israelites in Egypt to speak about the real world of Jews in the world today. These people, I think, find deeply troubling a principal side to their existence, so troubling that they invoke it, deny it, celebrate its end in ancient times, and fervently ask that it come to a conclusion once again. Obviously, it is not slavery. That freedom Jews celebrate—but also seek (so the liturgy maintains) from one thing, to do some other. Let us go back over the language of the Passover narrative once again:

> We were slaves . . . in Egypt . . . and if the Holy One . . . had not . . . , we would still be slaves.
>
> This year slaves here, next year free in Jerusalem.
>
> *In every generation they rise against us, and in every generation God delivers us.*
>
> For ever after, in every generation, every Israelite must think of himself or herself as having gone forth from Egypt.

Organized, socially acceptable paranoia? Not at all. Would that it were! The facts of the history of the Jews over the centuries transform paranoia into understatement. The phrase *In every generation they rise against us* . . . bears the message that enjoys self-evidence: we are we, and they hate us.

Now my full answer to the question, Why this? is evident: the key to the power of the Passover seder is found in the resentment expressed in the simple, and in my view, self-evidently true statement, "In every generation they rise against us." If I had to explain in one sentence why the extraordinary appeal of Passover, it is not in the mythic being invoked but in the this-worldly, factual statement: we are hated, we are in trouble, but God saves (or: something happens). Passover is popular now because it speaks to a generation that knows what the Gentiles can do, having seen what they did to the Jews of Europe.

Passover furthermore speaks not to history alone but to personal biography. It joins together history with the experience of the individual, because the individual as a minority finds self-evident—relevant, true, urgent—a rite that reaches into the everyday and the here and now and turns that common world into a metaphor for the reality of Israel, enslaved but also redeemed. Whether or not people see themselves as having gone forth from Egypt I cannot say. But I know that they see themselves as slaves in Egypt. And that is what draws them to the seder. It explains what, in the everyday, things mean beyond the four ells of the private person's world. In terms now familiar, the seder effects its enchantment by showing the individual that the everyday stands for something beyond; the here and now represent the everywhere and all the time: "In every generation they rise against us." True, but also, God saves. Who would not be glad to have supper to celebrate that truth, if only through commemoration.

If the Passover seder banquet enchants the everyday experience of people under pressure, transforming what is personal and private into what is public and shared, nothing in the unfolding of the seder rite focuses upon that one message. The words speak of many things, only occasionally coming to the main point. Not only so, but when they participate in a Passover seder, people bring with them more than a single resentment, and the pleasure of the occasion may obscure whatever resentment they may feel. But the words speak; the main point remains present throughout because that one theme—the Exodus of Israel from Egypt—remains at the fore. The word *seder* means "order," and the sense is that a sequence of actions takes place as prescribed. Here is the order of the seder. The word *matzah* refers to unleavened bread. What we shall see is that same disjuncture between the words and the deeds, the declarations and the inner sentiment. To make this clear I have divided the order into the gestures on one side and the recitation of words on the other:

Deeds	words
first washing of the hands	
eating of the parsley	
breaking of the middle cake of matzah	
	recital of the narrative
second washing of the hands	
	grace for bread
breaking and dividing up of topmost piece of matzah	
eating of bitter herb dipped in charoset (chopped nuts, wine)	
eating of bitter herb with matzah	
meal	
eating of the afikomon (a piece of matzah eaten to mark the end of the meal)	
	grace after the meal
	Hallel (recitation of Psalms 113-118)
	closing prayer

A curious picture emerges of two quite separate occasions, running side by side but not meeting. Were we to describe the banquet on the basis of this catalogue, we should expect a recitation much engaged by attention to hand washing, the eating of parsley, the breaking and disposition of pieces of unleavened bread—in all, raising and lowering, breaking and hiding and eating, pieces of matzah.

I should then be unprepared for the reality of the seder rite, which involves an enormous flow of words. Not only so, but the introit of the rite focuses upon the ritual aspect of the meal, not on the narrative:

> Why has this night been made different from all other nights? On all other nights we eat bread whether leavened or unleavened, on this night only unleavened; on all other nights we eat all kinds of herbs, on this night only bitter ones; on all other nights we do not dip herbs even once; on this night, twice; on all other nights we sit at the table either sitting or reclining, on this night we all recline.

In point of fact, none of these questions, addressed by the youngest present to the presiding officer, is ever answered. Instead we have the following (I italicize the operative words):

We were the slave of Pharaoh in Egypt; and the Lord our God brought us forth from there with a mighty hand and an outstretched arm. And if the Holy One, blessed be He, had not brought our fathers forth from Egypt, then surely we, and our children, and our children's children, would be enslaved to Pharaoh in Egypt. *And so, even if all of us were full of wisdom and understanding, well along in years and deeply versed in the tradition, we should still be bidden to repeat once more the story of the Exodus from Egypt; and he who delights to dwell on the liberation is one to be praised.*

We now shift from the symbols present to the occasion commemorated. By means of a considerable "narrative," we remember Pharaoh and Egypt. This narrative is composed of a citation and exegesis of some verses of Scripture, some games, prayers, snatches of stories, and hymns.

Made up of incoherent liturgies, joining together varieties of essentially unrelated materials, the so-called narrative tells the following story, and I take it to form the centerpiece of the whole:

Long ago our ancestors were idol-worshipers but now the Holy One has drawn us to his service. So we read in the Torah: "And Joshua said to all the people, 'Thus says the Lord, God of Israel: From time immemorial your fathers lived beyond the river Euphrates, even to Terah, father of Abraham and of Nahor, and they worshiped idols. And I took your father Abraham from beyond the river and guided his footsteps throughout the land of Canaan. I multiplied his offspring and gave him Isaac. To Isaac I gave Jacob and Esau. And I set apart Mount Seir as the inheritance of Esau, while Jacob and his sons went down to Egypt.' "

This takes place around a table, with family and friends. That our ancestors were idol worshipers does not pertain to the occasion. All of it is deeply relevant to those present, for it says who they really are, and for whom they really stand. They in the here and now stand for "our ancestors," Abraham, Isaac, and Jacob. The narrative continues:

Blessed is *he who keeps his promise to Israel . . . for the Holy One set a term to our bondage,* fulfilling the word which he gave our father Abraham in the covenant made between the divided sacrifice: "Know beyond a doubt that your offspring will be *strangers in a land that is not theirs,* four hundred years they shall serve and suffer. But in the end I shall pronounce judgment on the oppressor people and your offspring shall go forth with great wealth." (Key words emphasized.)

We are dealing here with people who respond to the description of their circumstance: strangers in a land that is not theirs indeed!

That is bad sociology, and, for the free Jews of the Western democracies, worse politics. But in the heart, it rings true: *strangers in a land that is not theirs,* not because their neighbors are enemies, but because they are different from their neighbors, and that suffices. Canada and America are as much theirs as anyone else's, but still they are *strangers.* They could, of course, migrate to a land that *is* theirs (within its civil myth), namely, the state of Israel. But they do not—and yet they say, "This year here, slaves, next year, free people in Jerusalem." There is a jarring unreality to the entire drama. Through the natural eye, one sees ordinary folk, not much different from their neighbors in dress, language, or aspirations. The words they speak do not describe reality and are not meant to. When Jewish people say of themselves, "We were the slaves of Pharaoh in Egypt," although they never felt the lash, through the eye of faith that is just what they have done. It is *their* liberation they now celebrate, not merely that of long-dead forebears.

The power of the Passover banquet rite is that it transforms ordinary existence into an account of something beyond. The ordinary existence imposes its tensions. Jews are different from Gentiles. That is what defines them as Jews. But now, in the transformation at hand, to be a Jew means to be a slave who has been liberated by God. To be Israel means to give eternal thanks for God's deliverance. And that deliverance is not at a single moment in historical time. Transformed into a permanent feature of reality, it is made myth, that story of deep truth that comes true in every generation and is always celebrated. Here again, events of natural, ordinary life are transformed through myth into paradigmatic, eternal, and ever recurrent sacred moments. In terms we have used before, the everyday is treated as a paradigm and a metaphor. Jews think of themselves as having gone forth from Egypt, and Scripture so instructs them. God did not redeem the dead generation of the Exodus alone, but the living too—especially the living. Thus the family states:

> Again and again, in double and redoubled measure, are we beholden to God the All-Present: that He freed us from the Egyptians and wrought His judgment on them; that He sentenced all their idols and slaughtered all their firstborn; that He gave their treasure to us and split the Red Sea for us; that He led us through it dry shod and drowned the tyrants in it;

that He helped us through the desert and fed us with the manna; that He gave the Sabbath to us and brought us to Mount Sinai; that He gave the Torah to us and brought us to our homeland—there to build the Temple for us, for atonement of our sins.

Israel was born in historical times. Historians, biblical scholars, and archaeologists have much to say about that event. But to the classical Jew their findings, while interesting, have little bearing on the meaning of reality. The redemptive promise that stood by the forefathers and "stands by us" is not a mundane historical event, but a mythic interpretation of historical, natural events. Oppression, homelessness, extermination—like salvation, homecoming, renaissance—are this-worldly and profane, supplying headlines for newspapers. The myth that a Jew must think of himself or herself as having gone forth from Egypt and as being redeemed by God renders ordinary experience into a moment of celebration. If "us, too, the living, He [has] redeemed," then the observer no longer witnesses only historical men in historical time, but an eternal return to sacred time.

Having come this far, we cannot evade the issue implicit in celebration of the Exodus: how long, when, and by whom? That is to say, the enchantment transforms not only the here and now of the meal; it changes the view of time ahead, the age beyond. For what, after all, does the seder have to say about Israel's ongoing history? Is it merely a succession of meaningless disasters—worldly happenings without end or purpose? The answer comes in a folk song sung at the Passover seder:

> An only kid, an only kid
> My father bought for two pennies,
> An only kid, an only kid.
> But along came the cat and ate up the kid
> My father bought for two pennies,
> An only kid, an only kid.

And so goes the dreary story. Here is the final verse:

> Then the Holy One, blessed be He, came along
> And slew the angel of death
> Who slew the slaughterer

Who slew the ox
Who drank the water
That put out the fire
That burned the stick
That beat the dog
That bit the cat
That ate the kid
My father had bought for two pennies,
An only kid, an only kid.

The history of the Jewish people is the history of the only kid. In the end, the Holy One, blessed be He, comes to slaughter the angel of death, vindicate the long sufferings of many centuries, and bring to a happy and joyful end the times of trouble.

Here is the whole of Israel's history embodied in the little lamb the father bought for next to nothing, his only kid. Here once more is that public, legitimate, organized paranoia that corresponds to awful reality: what has happened to the Jews turns paranoia into understatement. No wonder the resentment, the fear, the uncertainty, and no wonder the annual assembly to celebrate what "we" really are and how "we" really feel.

The fate of Israel—the lamb slaughtered not once but many times over—is suffering that has an end and a purpose in the end of days. Death will die, and all who shared in the lamb's suffering will witness the divine denouement of history. The history of sin, suffering, atonement, and reconciliation is a cycle not destined to repeat itself forever.

To hear such a message—deriving from and yet transcending one's everyday experience—will people not gladly come for supper? What unites the discrete, unrelated events in the life of the "only kid" and provokes a singular response among varied men is the pervasive conviction that an end *is* coming. Nothing is meaningless, for the random happenings of the centuries are in truth leading to the Messiah. The messianic hope lies at the end of the mythic life of Israel and illuminates every moment in it. People may not perceive meaning in what happens to them in their everyday lives, but they want to. That is why the magic works. It is made to work by the power of the will and the force of the imagination which match the world as experienced with the world as explained. The will and imagination transform time from now to history, change space from here to there, turn action from resentment or fear of the outsider to slavery then freedom, and—above all—transform community made up out of family and friends, into Israel. The Passover seder finds nearly all Jews in America and Canada, whether they call themselves religious or secular, around the banquet table. Its curious message speaks to us all. But then, on the morrow, when the synagogue opens its door, most Jews find themselves somewhere else. That puzzling act of selectivity will demand its explanation in due course.

◇———————————————————————————◇

Hanukkah

Hanukkah, the festival of consecration, observed in December, enjoys enormous popularity, and not only among Jews. In the Tampa Bay area, where I live, scarcely 1% of the population is Jewish. Yet why do television stations wish everybody Merry Christmas and Happy Hanukkah, as though the proportions of the population that keep the two festivals are approximately even? (They ignore Kwanzaa, the American black post-Christmas rites, though blacks greatly outnumber Jews in West Central Florida.) The reason, of course, is that Hanukkah is "the Jewish Christmas," and at that season of goodwill, people are eager to include everybody. And they do.

Hanukkah at any other season would be ignored, but at this season it is prized. The rites are simple enough—an additional paragraph added to the daily prayers—which few recite; an additional Scriptural lection in synagogue worship—which few attend; a nightly lighting of a candle over eight nights—and this everybody does. Along with the lighting, there is the shower of gifts, and everybody takes a bath in pure sentimentality. Observed as an add-on in synagogues and temples, Hanukkah is celebrated in every Jewish family that has children.

In this context, the popularity of Hanukkah is readily explained. In times past a minor festival, it has come to the fore because of three facts. First, it is celebrated at home, with family. The central rite—the lighting of the Hanukkah candles for eight nights—and the singing of songs bring parents together with children. Second, it bears the message

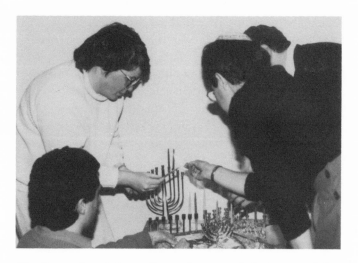

Family members light candles on the menorah during one of the
eight nights of Hanukkah.

of defiance—the few against the many, the holy against the profane—
and victory over oppression that Jews find congenial. And, third, it
comes at the right time of year, when, overwhelmed with Christmas,
Jews find something of their own to celebrate. Why this, not that?
"Blessed are you, Lord, our God, ruler of the world, who did miracles
for our ancestors in those days at this season." And what a miracle:
something Jewish in December, the loneliest time in the year for people
who love the everyday world of the streets and gathering places of
America. The message of Hanukkah for Jews is self-evident. Resist the
majority culture as did our heroic ancestors. But all you have to do to
be heroic is stay Jewish—that's all it takes, whatever it means.

CHAPTER 5

What Defines the Self-Evidence of the Judaic Rites of Passage?

Circumcision, the Bar or Bat Mitzvah, Marriage, and Death

◇

When it comes to rites of passage, the proportion of Jews who observe the requirements of Judaism is greater than the proportion that does not, and, at each point, we ask why, and why not? The answer is, what is personal is practiced, what is communal is not. And why, even when vast numbers of people observe a rite, do they not necessarily observe the rite in accord with the requirements of the law of Judaism? Because the law is public, communal, authoritative, and what people do, they do by reason of their personal decision. Law requires a sense of obligation—in the context of Judaism, of covenant with God. But the faith, so Protestant at its core, imposes only the priority of personal meaning: this I find meaningful, so I do it, in the way I find it meaningful—even though what I do has no relationship to what Judaism says I should do. Our survey of rites of passage—what they are, and why and how they are carried out—proves more extensive than those of the rites of home and synagogue that are broadly practiced.

◇——————————————————————————————◇

Circumcision

Most male Jews born in North America are circumcised. For some, the operation constitutes a religious rite, carried out by a properly trained ritual circumciser (*mohel*). For others the rite is done by a physician in the hospital, with no religious rite at all. While, according to the books, that makes all the difference (If it is not done by a mohel, it is not a religious rite and does not fulfill the commandment of circumcision into the covenant), for sizable numbers of Judaists, it makes no difference at all. It is the rite that counts. As we recall, while only a third of the grandparents care that their grandchildren are raised as Jews, half want their grandsons to be circumcised. The notion of circumcising a grandson who is, by Jewish law, a Gentile is incomprehensible to the law of Judaism; Gentiles do not have to be circumcised, and if they are, that by itself does not make them Jews.[1] No one ever claimed that what the people do forms so coherent and harmonious a religious system as the one the books set forth!

That inconsistency presents the problem of making sense of circumcision not in the books but in the peoples' practice. If the rite were (nearly) universal but also carried out in accord with the Torah, our method would suffice to explain why this. If the rite were largely ignored, we should have data to explain why not that. But where the rite is apparently broadly practiced, but in so diverse a set of ways that we cannot claim that the words answer a question that people are asking, interpreting the popularity of the rite proves parlous. And yet, the fact[2] of the popular acceptance of the rite speaks for itself.

Why this in this particular way? Numerous Judaists choose the surgical operation for the rite, content to have a rite of passage performed—but where they are not present (in a hospital). The "why this" of circumcision then is simple: it is a fundamental rite of passage. The how of the "why this" is equally apparent: it is, after all, a blood rite, and performing the act of circumcision in a religious setting, with prayers said and then the foreskin removed, makes people (particularly males) confront the stark, naked reality of the faith—blood and flesh and all. But for the generality of Judaists, that is not quite what they have in

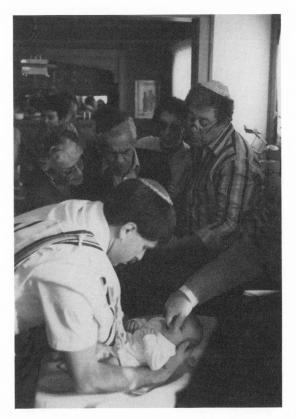

Grandparents recite traditional prayers as a mohel
performs the circumcision rite. A finger is dipped in
wine and placed in the baby's mouth.

mind. Those Judaists—and I suspect they are very many—translate
wanting to be Jewish but not too Jewish into a very simple procedure:
to do it with their eyes closed. For the rite is not to be disguised, its
full, uncompromising, utterly physical character, not to be dissimulated.

There is another aspect to consider: the myth that accompanies the
rite. If, as I claim, the words people say matter, then the disjuncture
between what the people practice and the unanimous prescriptions of
the holy books ought to tell us something about why things are done
the way they are. When we do, then, we identify a further pretense,
rendering implausible a rite that people find urgent. For (as usual) the
words of enchantment transform the birth of the child to the parents—

from a private and personal happening in the natural family to a public and momentous event in the life of the supernatural family of Israel on earth and of God in heaven. People find it easy to identify with God's freeing of Israel from Egyptian slavery because of their experience of the social world. But the mythic setting of the rite of circumcision invokes an identification with no clear point of correspondence with the contemporary social circumstance of holy Israel. For people understand resentment but not covenant. (I shall return to this point in chapter 7.) The circumcision that carries the infant boy into the covenant of Abraham imposes the obligations of the covenant and its responsibilities, and what the people do, they do because they want to—choosing what they find meaningful, ignoring what is merely obligatory. Circumcision and covenant contradict a votive religion. So far as people hear the words they say,[3] they cannot listen to them. Better to let a surgeon do it in a hospital, when nothing is at stake but the deed itself.

Specifically, in the case of a male child, a minor surgical rite—one of limited or even dubious medical value—becomes the mark of the renewal of the agreement between God and Israel, the covenant carved into the flesh of every Jewish male. The beginning of a new life renews the rule that governs Israel's relationship to God. So the private joy is reworked through words of enchantment—once more, sanctification—and so transformed into renewal of the community of Israel and God. And the last thing the people want when it comes to the rites the books prescribe is a community, whether of holy Israel or of Israel and God. That is not exactly what they have in mind.

The rite of passage of circumcision in Judaism therefore takes a most personal moment, the birth of a child through private sexual union of the mother and the father and the personal travail of the mother (which is never mentioned in the rite). That most individual occasion, the beginning of a person's life, links in a concrete way to specific moments and personalities in the public and supernatural life of Israel. When, at the frontier between life and life, the faith intervenes, people let loose the reins of imagination. In the case of the Jewish son, they perform a surgical operation in the name of the faith, calling the rite *berit milah,* the covenant of or effected through the rite of circumcision. *Berit milah* seals with the blood of the infant son the contract between Israel and God, generation by generation.

Now to the portrait given in the books.[4] Circumcision must take place on the eighth day after birth, normally in the presence of a quorum of ten adult males. Very commonly, it is done in the home in the company of relatives and friends. There is nothing private nor merely surgical about the operation. The contemporary practice of having a surgical operation in no way fulfills the rite of circumcision. What qualifies it as a rite is not only circumstance. It is the formula, the words of blessing that form the counterpart to the grace after meals. It is the medium of enchantment that transforms the birth of a child into an event heavy with meaning; a metaphor for something more.

Psychologically this is quite natural. For no moment in the passage of life from birth to death so touches a parent as does the birth of a child. Questions of past and future weigh heavily on the present. The parents look backward, toward family, perhaps for a time (as young people find expedient) neglected prior to the advent of the son. They direct hopes forward, toward a future of perfection to be realized by the child, a perfection, of course, unattained by the parents themselves and likely unattainable by any mortal. So great is the power of dreaming. Fathers and mothers now become grandparents; siblings become uncles and aunts. A new social entity takes shape around the new person. When, on such an occasion, Judaism intervenes, exhausted mother and happy, confused father will do pretty much whatever they are told in the name of a blessing for the child (if only *mazal tov*, meaning, "under a good star").

When the rite begins, the assembly and the mohel together recite the following:

> The Lord spoke to Moses saying, Phineas, son of Eleazar, son of Aaron, the priest, has turned my wrath from the Israelites by displaying among them his passion for me, so that I did not wipe out the Israelite people in my passion. Say therefore I grant him my covenant of peace.

Commenting on this passage, Lifsa Schachter wrote, "Phineas is identified with zealously opposing the . . . sins of sexual licentiousness and idolatry. He is best known for an event which occurred when the Israelites, whoring with Moabite women in the desert, were drawn to the worship of Baal-Peor. . . . Phineas leaped into the fray and through an act of double murder . . . quieted God's terrible wrath."[5] Needless to say, a figure who stands for zeal will present a question to the peoples' program; it is one thing to admire Judah Maccabee, the hero of Hanukkah, who fought the Greeks for the Jews' right to "be different," and not worship idols (as the story of the festival goes). The Maccabees stand for what the people have in mind during the Christmas season— resisting an intrusive, alien world. It is quite another thing to admire a zealot who extirpated heresy; for if there is heresy, there are norms, and if norms, then obligations. A religion of home and family but not community recognizes what is meaningful, therefore once more, votive, but not what is obligatory. Phineas is a fine choice for the rite of circumcision into the covenant, blood and all. No wonder, again, perhaps by instinct, any number of "good Jews" want the result of the rite but without the blood.

In the room where the rite takes place, there is a chair called "the chair of Elijah." The newborn son is set on that chair, and the congregation says, "This is the chair of Elijah, of blessed memory." Here is the second hero of the occasion. Elijah had complained to God that Israel neglected the covenant (1 Kings 19:10-14). So he comes to bear witness that Israel observes the covenant of circumcision. To understand the invocation of Elijah, for whom a chair is set, we first recall the pertinent biblical passage:

> Then the word of the Lord came to him, saying, "What are you doing here, Elijah?" He answered, "I have been very zealous for the Lord, the God of hosts; for the Israelites have forsaken your covenant, thrown down your altars, and killed your prophets with the sword. I alone am left, and they are seeking my life, to take it away." He said, "Go out and stand on the mountain before the Lord, for the Lord is about to pass by." Now there was a great wind, so strong that it was splitting mountains and breaking rocks in pieces before the Lord, but the Lord was not in the wind; and after the wind an earthquake, but the Lord was not in the earthquake; and after the earthquake a fire, but the Lord was not in the fire; and after the fire a sound of sheer silence. When Elijah heard it, he wrapped his face in his mantle and went out and stood at the entrance of the cave. Then there came a voice to him that said, "What are you doing here, Elijah?" He answered, "I have been very zealous for the Lord, the God of hosts; for the Israelites have forsaken your covenant, thrown down your altars, and killed your prophets with the sword. I alone am left, and they are seeking my life, to take it away."
>
> (1 Kings 19:9b-14 NRSV)

"I alone am left" indeed! To what social circumstance can Elijah correspond, and what experience in this world does Elijah evoke? People do not crave a circumstance or an experience. A martyr-people is not what they want to form.

This passage stands behind the story told in a medieval document, *Pirke deRabbi Eliezer*:[6]

The Israelites were wont to circumcise until they were divided into two kingdoms. The kingdom of Ephraim cast off from themselves the covenant of circumcision. Elijah, may he be remembered for good, arose and was zealous with a mighty passion, and he adjured the heavens to send down neither dew nor rain upon the earth. Jezebel heard about it and sought to slay him.

Elijah arose and prayed before the Holy One, blessed be he. The Holy One, blessed be he, said to him, "Are you better than your fathers?" (1 Kgs. 19:4). Esau sought to slay Jacob, but he fled before him, as it is said, "And Jacob fled into the field of Aram" (Hos. 12:12).

Pharaoh sought to slay Moses, who fled before him and he was saved, as it is said, "Now when Pharaoh heard this thing, he sought to slay Moses. And Moses fled from the face of Pharaoh" (Ex. 2:15).

Saul sought to slay David, who fled before him and was saved, as it is said, "If you save not your life tonight, tomorrow you will be killed" (1 Sam. 19:11).

Another text says, "And David fled and escaped" (1 Sam. 19:18). Learn that everyone who flees is remembered.

Elijah, may he be remembered for good, arose and fled from the land of Israel, and he betook himself to Mount Horeb, as it is said, "And he arose and ate and drank" (1 Kgs. 19:8).

Then the Holy One, blessed be he, was revealed to him and said to him, "What are you doing here, Elijah?"

He answered him saying, "I have been very zealous."

The Holy One, blessed be he, said to him, "You are always zealous. You were zealous in Shittim on account of the immorality. For it is said, 'Phineas, the son of Eleazar, the son of Aaron the priest, turned my wrath away from the children of Israel, in that he was zelaous with my zeal among them' (Num. 25:11). Here you are also zealous, by your life! They shall not observe the covenant of circumcision until you see it done with your own eyes."

Hence the sages have instituted the custom that people should have a seat of honor for the messenger of the covenant, for Elijah, may he be remembered for good, is called the messenger of the covenant, as it is said, "And the messenger of the covenant, whom you delight in, behold he comes" (Mal. 3:1).

So too the "messenger of the *covenant*" (Mal. 1:23) is the prophet Elijah, and he is present whenever a Jewish son enters the *covenant* of Abraham, which is circumcision. God therefore ordered him to come to every circumcision to witness the loyalty of the Jews to the covenant. Elijah then serves as the guardian for the newborn, just as he raised the child of the widow from the dead (1 Kings 17:17-24). Along these same lines, at the seder table of Passover, a cup of wine is poured for Elijah, and the door is opened for Elijah to join in the rite. Setting a seat for Elijah serves to invoke the presence of the guardian of the newborn and the zealous advocate of the rite of the circumcision of the covenant. Celebrating with the family of the newborn are not "all Israel" in general, but a very specific personage indeed. The gesture of setting the chair silently sets the stage for an event in the life of the family—not of the child alone but of all Israel. The chair of Elijah, filled by the one who holds the child, sets the newborn baby into Elijah's lap. The enchantment extends through the furnishing of the room; what is not ordinarily present is introduced, and that makes all the difference.

We move from gesture to formula. There is the blessing recited before the rite itself. As the mohel takes the knife to cut the foreskin, these words are said:

> Praised are You ... who sanctified us with Your commandments and commanded us to bring the son into the covenant of Abraham our father.

The third hero of the rite is, of course, Abraham, with whom circumcision into the covenant commenced. The explicit invocation of Abraham's covenant turns the concrete action in the here and now into a simile of the paradigm and archetype: I circumcise my son just as Abraham circumcised Isaac and Ishmael. Then I am a father, like Abraham, and—more to the point—my fatherhood is like Abraham's.

Then the operation is carried out.

Following the operation, the wine is blessed, introducing yet a further occasion of enchantment:

Praised are You, Lord our God, who sanctified the beloved from the womb and set a statute into his very flesh, and his parts sealed with the sign of the holy covenant. On this account, Living God, our portion and rock, save the beloved of our flesh from destruction, for the sake of his covenant placed in our flesh. Blessed are You . . . who make the covenant.

The covenant is not a generality; it is specific, concrete, fleshly. Moreover, it is meant to accomplish a very specific goal—as all religion means to attain concrete purposes—to secure a place for the child, a blessing for the child. By virtue of the rite, the child enters the covenant, meaning that he joins that unseen "Israel" that through blood enters an agreement with God. Then the blessing of the covenant is owing to the child. For covenants or contracts cut both ways.

After the father has recited the blessing, ". . . who has sanctified us by his commandments and has commanded us to induct him into the covenant of our father, Abraham," the community responds: "Just as he has entered the covenant, so may he be introduced to Torah, the *huppah* [marriage canopy] and good deeds." Schachter comments on this passage as follows:

> In the presence of Elijah . . . *Torah*—as against idolatry; in the presence of Phineas . . . *huppah*, as against sexual licentiousness; in the presence of Abraham . . . to *good deeds*: *For I have singled him out that he may instruct his children and his posterity to keep the way of the Lord by doing what is just and right* (Gen. 18:18).[7]

Now to return to our question, why do so many people practice the rite but not in the way the books prescribe? When the rite is one of passage or involves home and family, people are glad to carry it out; when the books invoke for the rite the sentiment of community and attitudes of obligation, people cannot hear or do not want to. So the happy compromise: let a surgeon do it. What has happened here is that the "I" of the personal rite of passage becomes the "we" of holy Israel, embodied in the here and now in the "I" of this father and mother, this son, this assembled family and these members of the community of Israel. That is why, if I had to explain the (evidently) wide disjuncture between the practice of the rite and the practice of the rite in the way the books describe, I should say the rite is done because the peoples' Judaism focuses upon rites of passage. But the rite is not invariably done in accord with the way the books say because the people find implausible the message of the liturgy. And why should that be the case? If they can be slaves escaping from Egypt, why not witnesses to Elijah's presence? The one is no less plausible than the other. But the social experience of Jews in North American society imparts relevance, even immediacy, to the metaphor of slaves and Pharaoh. But nothing in the social order prepares them for the knife and the chair of Elijah. Perhaps people cannot stand too much reality, and the mixture of covenant and blood in elevated images bears a certain eloquence, but on the dining room table, repels.

But for holy Israel, blood should not repel, and that is for a reason particular to our own time. The rite of circumcision stands for the continuity of family in Israel. The prominence of that rite of passage in peoples' minds—despite its mythic improbability—derives from that deep will to say to the past and to the future: here I am, here we come. Now, for vast numbers of North American Jews, coming to America represents the severing of all ties to the past. I do not mean, when the immigrants came some generations ago, they lost contact with Yiddish or German and spoke American or Canadian English (or French). Nor do I mean, coming to America marked the end of traditional observance, although for many, to be an American meant to eat if not bacon then at least shrimp and scallops, and ultimately, lobster.

What I mean is more immediate. Families with continuing ties to European branches, in Poland or what was the USSR or Romania or Hungary or Germany, in World War II lost all their relatives. For those families, there is no physical past, no village where it all began, no house to go home to see. New Zealanders of English origin go home to the houses in which their great-great-great grandparents lived. The families may be there; the houses often are. No North American Jew can go back to the village in Poland or Belarus or the Ukraine where their family lived for centuries—but only to Auschwitz. That is where the North American Jewish past came to an end; it is why there is no past, except in rite. So why should blood repel, when blood is all there is, and when, after all, it all ended in blood. The reality of life is not only death but continuation for the generations; it is also a different death, a meaner one. The blood of the covenant is right and true: the covenant really was, and remains, a covenant of blood, in all senses and aspects.

◇───────────────────────────────────────◇

Bar and Bat Mitzvah

A bloodless rite, bar mitzvah, for boys, and bat mitzvah, for girls, find nearly unanimous practice among Judaists.[8] Rites of passage carry from circumcision to puberty, and here, in the United States and Canada, girls as well as boys are celebrated. The single most important rite in contemporary Judaism in North America is the celebration of puberty, for boys among the Orthodox, for boys and girls among Conservative, Reform, and Reconstructionist, which is to say, nearly all Jews. So much for what the people do.

It is an intensely personal and familial rite, and it has taken over the synagogue and turned public worship into a private celebration. People who are not invited to a bar mitzvah that is celebrated on a Sabbath morning in a synagogue feel out of place at public worship. And rightly so. The family takes over the synagogue, and that is why the rite is a synagogue rite at all. One common ritual is for the Torah to be removed from the ark by the oldest member of the family and to be handed on, generation by generation, down to the bar or bat mitzvah child. Needless to say, this is accompanied by a vast amount of bathos and sentimentality. At a bar mitzvah I attended, the rabbi, whose son was called to the Torah as a bar mitzvah that day, delivered his sermon to his son, crying from beginning to end. It was, to say the least, embarrassing to many present. But in the synagogues, such public displays of emotions are required: the bar mitzvah replicates the emotions of the funeral. And well it does, since it celebrates, very commonly, the conclusion of such little "Jewish education" as the bar or bat mitzvah child ever is going to receive. It is not without reason that it marks as fundamentally pediatric the synagogue Judaism of America.

The books say very little about the matter and hardly prepare us for such a rite. True, from the earliest documents, beginning with the Mishnah (ca. 200 C.E.) forward, the books recognize that along with puberty comes responsibility for one's own actions, and that applies to girls at twelve and boys at thirteen. It is equally true that for a long time some sort of minor celebration has accompanied the first time a boy was called to read from the Torah in synagogue services. But this

A thirteen-year-old Jewish boy celebrates his bar mitzvah with relatives.

rite of passage has become in North America a towering occasion, celebrated in ways and proportions that the holy books cannot have prepared us to anticipate; and celebrated for girls as much as for boys, which the holy books do not know at all. Here is a case in which what separates the peoples' ways from the books' words is not neglect but the opposite: disproportion.

My explanation of the persistence of the rite remains simple: rites of passage endure. Some diminish in public character, as in the case of circumcision, and some grow in public esteem, as in the case of the bar or bat mitzvah, and this is in proportion to the relevance of the answer to the question that they give—but also, the plausibility of the answer. Circumcision evokes too much reality; the celebration of bar or bat mitzvah permits people to make up their own reality—and so to the bar part of the bar mitzvah.

Let us examine the rite itself. It is, in fact, in its actuality so uncomplicated that, by comparison to the dense presences at the circumcision, it scarcely seems a rite at all. When a child reaches puberty (for males, thirteen; for females, twelve or thirteen), he or she is called for the first time to the Torah. What happens at the bar or bat mitzvah? The young person is called to the Torah, recites the blessing that is required prior to the public proclamation of a passage of the Torah, and reads that passage (or stands as it is read). When the Torah lection of the week has been read, the congregation proceeds to a passage of the prophets. The young person reads that passage for the congregation. That is the rite—no rite at all.

It really is no rite simply because nothing is done on that occasion that is not done by others on the same occasion and that the boy or girl will not do a week later, with no further celebration. The young person is treated no differently from others that Sabbath, or last week, or next week. He or she simply assumes a place within the congregation of adult Jews, is counted for a quorum, and is expected to carry out the religious duties that pertain. The young person is not asked to imagine himself or herself in some mythic state or setting (in Eden or at Sinai or in the Jerusalem of the Messiah's time). The family of the young person does not find itself compared to "all Israel," and no stories are told about how the young person and the family reenact the mythic event, for instance, of the Exodus of Egypt. No one is commanded to see himself or herself as if this morning he or she was born, crossed the Red Sea, entered the Promised Land, or did any of those other things that the story of the dual Torah invokes on enchanted occasions of personal transformation.

Indeed, it is, on the whole, a bloodless and rather impersonal trans-action, the only thing changing being the status of the child. A bar mitzvah or bat mitzvah is "one who is subject to the requirement of carrying out religious deeds, one who bears responsibility for himself or herself." That simple transaction—coming for the first time as an adult to assume the rights and responsibilities of maturity—forms the single most powerful occasion in the life of the maturing young Jew and his or her family. It is prepared for, celebrated rather elaborately, looked back upon as a highlight of life. But all that has changed is that the week before the youngster could not be called to the Torah to say a blessing before the Torah is read to the community at synagogue worship, and the week after, he or she can and will be called up.

Only when a Jew achieves intelligence and self-consciousness, nor-mally at puberty, is he or she expected to accept the full responsibility of *mitzvah* (commandment) and to regard himself or herself as *com-manded* by God. But that sense of "being commanded" is impersonal and not imposed by the invocation of a myth. The transaction is neutral; it involves affirmation and assent, confirmation and commitment. But there is no bower, no Eden (as in the marriage rite we shall examine in the next section of this chapter), no family at table reading a received rite (as in the Passover rite).

Judaism perceives the commandments as expressions of one's acceptance of the yoke of the kingdom of heaven and submission to God's will. That acceptance cannot be coerced, but requires thoughtful and complete affirmation. The bar or bat mitzvah thus represents the moment that the young Jew first assumes full responsibility before God to keep the commandments. Calling the young person to the Torah and conferring upon him or her the rights of a full member of the community ratify what has taken place. Those actions do not effect a change in status of the individual, all the more so a significant alteration in the condition of the community.

This fact carries us to a reconsideration of the theory I offer in these pages, that the rites that people celebrate are those of home and family, individual but not community. But then, we see a striking contrast in the premise of choice, between the givens of the Judaism people practice, and the datum of the Judaism set forth by the books. Why no rites at all for death and puberty? Because these are totally individual experiences. That is why there can be no appeal to "Israel" with its holy life worldview. The radically isolated individual cannot be Israel. So we saw in the liturgy for the Day of Atonement, a day on which the individual atones for his or her sins, but in the language, "we."

The reason is that the smallest whole unit of an Israel begins with family (or its surrogate), that is, with a shared past. That is why birth undergoes the transformation of circumcision, which links the newborn boy child (and, today, synagogue rites encompass the girl child as well) to the increment of Israel. Marriage too is a family event, in which holy Israel has a stake in a way in which in death it does not. What makes the difference? Puberty marks no change in the makeup of the community, since the child enters the community at birth and never leaves. Puberty marks merely a shift in the status of an individual, who becomes responsible to the community and to its norms, to God and to God's will.

Death is left unaffected by the transforming power of enchanted words because, in the most profound sense, words cannot change what has happened, and because, for that same reason, the one who dies dies alone, within the family, while the community goes forward unimpaired.

The social entity (nation, holy people, community) takes note, communities celebrate puberty and commemorate death, but community is unchanged—it goes on, augmented by bar mitzvah, diminished by death, essentially intact. There is only one aspect of death that, within the received Torah, comes under the aspect of transformation, and that is the one side to matters that profoundly affects the community, as we shall see in a moment. We shall first attend to the simpler of the two matters, the absence of a ring of rites surrounding puberty, with which we are now familiar.

And yet, the bar or bat mitzvah is a magnificent, often regal occasion, celebrated with vigor and enthusiasm by Jews who otherwise do not often find their way to the synagogue on Sabbath mornings: Jews married to Gentiles, Jews themselves not "barmitzved," Jews remote from any and all connection with Jewish organizations, institutions, activities, observances. Why? First, it is an occasion for dinners and dances, lavish expenditure on an open bar and a huge meal (hence the standard joke about "too much bar and not enough mitzvah"). Second and more to the point, many Jews find the occasion intensely meaningful, deeply affecting. And that has nothing to do with either the bar or the mitzvah. It is something else.

Like the rite of circumcision, which may be all circumcision and no rite, so bar or bat mitzvah today celebrates continuity, tests the strength of the chain of generations and confirms its endurance. At a bar or bat mitzvah, a parent thinks not so much of the future as of the past, especially if a grandparent or parent is deceased. The entire family assembles, and that is as much the past as the future. I remember, myself, how deeply moving my firstborn's bar mitzvah was for my wife and me. No ratiocination prepared me for the intense emotion of the moment. It was so profound it reminded me of only three other occasions in my life, the moment my wife accepted my marriage proposal and standing at the graveside of my father and, thirteen years later, my father-in-law, watching their bodies buried in the ground. Union in love, reunion with the dirt—these mark the turnings of life. But a child's bar or bat mitzvah?

In order to account for these deep feelings, I appeal to the fear—commonplace in Jews who lived through the Holocaust—that they are at the end of the line. As I said earlier, for most American and Canadian Jewish families of European origin, there is no past before America or

Canada. So there is a deep sense in which our own generation marks the turning, either downward or toward an open future. And the choice is made for life every time a bar or bat mitzvah is celebrated. We must remember that Jews have no past, since the Jews who perished in Europe included pretty much all of the families of Jews now alive in the West (excluding only those who come from the Muslim world, where Jews of course endured for centuries). Not only so, but if one's family is two or three generations old in America, whether or not there was a family in Europe no one really knows, for there is no past beyond the grand-parents or great-grandparents who immigrated.

My grandmother came from somewhere in the northwest Ukraine or southwest Belarus. She knew what she left behind, and whom she left behind. I never did, and my father never did. He grew up in Beverly and had aunts and uncles all over the north shore of Boston, from Peabody and Lynn and Marblehead to Lowell and Haverill. That was his family—one generation old. On his father's side, he might as well have come from Jupiter. There was no one. So for me, there is one grandmother, and no past, and for my children, there are only two prior generations whom they know; no more whose names I know. This story of one family stands for the tale of many families: no past, prior to the immigrant generation, no past outside of America. The Jews conjure a long history for their people, but no genealogy for themselves. The bar or bat mitzvah forms the remedy to that sense of loss and absence. It forms a past; it points toward a future. The newly mature young woman or man is the link. There is continuity and hope. And that really is something to celebrate, and it is why, I think, even in the absence of rite, people invent rituals of bar or bat mitzvah celebration and spend more than they can afford to carry out those rituals.

There is yet another side to matters. The young boy or girl spends years preparing to participate in the rite. If for the mother and father the occasion evokes deep feelings of closed-off past and unmarked future, for the child it is still more affecting. To explain why, let me tell my own story. When I was a boy in West Hartford and had entered seventh grade, my father allowed me to go to afternoon Hebrew classes at a nearby Orthodox synagogue. It was only for that year. After becoming a bar mitzvah, the beginning of the following year, I worked in my father's newspaper office every afternoon after school, as well as Saturday mornings, through the end of high school. But in that prepubescent year I met, for the first and only time before mature years, that realm of the Torah that later on defined my being. One day, walking to Hebrew class, which I vastly enjoyed, I began to wonder what would happen when my father—"my" rabbi—died. Then I would be the last Jew on earth—I and maybe my best friend, Eddy. I could not let it be that way. So I decided to become a rabbi. From then to now a straight line stretched forward. My thinking was, I could not be the last Jew on earth. I had to replace my father—but I would be a better Jew than he was. I would know things. And I did. But not what my father knew—different things.

Jews in America—Jews without a past and without a well-planned future—fear that the Jews are dying out. They do not want to be the last Jews on earth. That fear and the hope it represents come to full and complete statement in the bar or bat mitzvah. We declare that we, the parents, are not the last Jews on earth. So why not celebrate? Thus, an intensely personal and familial occasion forms the centerpiece for a wildly popular rite—one for which the Judaism of the dual Torah has supplied no myth, no ritual, no medium of enchantment. But the world too enchants, and its hopes and fears transform.

◇————————————————————————————◇

The Marriage Rite

Without statistical evidence to lend weight to my impression, in general, when Judaists wed, it is a Judaic rite.[9] And when Jews die, ordinarily they are buried with the rites of Judaism.[10] It is exceedingly uncommon for one Jew to marry another in a secular ceremony,[11] and still less likely for a Judaist to marry another outside the faith (e.g., two Jews married by a Methodist minister). My own impression is that it is still less common for Jews to bury their dead with a secular rite; a rabbi is nearly always wanted. Why is it self-evident to people that, on the occasion of marriage and death, the book Judaism works? And why, furthermore, is it common for the rites of Judaism to be carried out according to the received rules? While the rite of circumcision gives way to a mere surgical procedure, the marriage ceremony, celebrated under a marriage canopy (called a huppah and therefore itself called a huppah), is ordinarily acted out within the framework of the received liturgy.

Perhaps the reason is that it is bloodless, and the antiseptic character appeals to American and Canadian Jews. But something else comes into play: the words of the liturgy itself, the actions that are taken. And here we have to ask, what accounts for the correspondence between the book rite and the practiced rite in the case of the huppah, which also explains the broadening gap between the book rite and the practiced rite in the case of circumcision? In both rites of passage (the one invokes, the other denies), it is the book Judaism that governs.

A preliminary hypothesis, resting on the character of the myth that accompanies the rite, points toward the difference between the humanly neutral Adam and Eve, to whom we compare the bridal couple, under the huppah, and the intensely Israelite and very particular Elijah—the exceedingly ethnic invocation of Abraham—called to witness the circumcision. So far as North American Jews want to be Jewish, but not too Jewish—not so Jewish that they cannot also fit into the larger society—circumcision without Abraham and Elijah (and without gentile friends, who are not commonly invited to the home rite) fits. "A good Jew" can have a son circumcised by a surgeon, so the consensus of behavior suggests. But a marriage rite with Adam and Eve before us—to that, myth and all, people can accommodate, and also invite platoons of gentile friends to celebrate as well. My impression is[12] that when a couple weds, they gladly include their gentile friends; when a few years later they celebrate their male child, the presence of these same friends is not required. Now consider the myth and see what I conceive to be the reason why: everyone can enjoy the celebration of Adam and Eve in Eden. For here is a Judaism for a nonsectarian world such as Jews want to imagine for themselves (and everybody else).

The huppah creates a nice illusion, matching the moment. For the beginning of a marriage itself takes place in a lovely fantasy. The bride plans to change the groom, the groom hopes the bride will never change—a grand illusion. And the transformation is not merely an exchange of illusions. Facts change, so far as attitudes and social norms define, also, concrete facts. We say words that legitimate what aforetimes was not (or, these days, at least, not in the same way). That change in a this-worldly sense is merely legal, a change in personal status and consequent property rights and obligations. But, in the enchantment of

Judaism, the words transform not only the relationship in law but also the participants (in our Western context) in love. In this way, as in the imaginative rereading of birth of a male baby, the "we" of you and me becomes the "us" of the social entity. But what "us" and which entity?

Entry into the imaginative world created by the rite of marriage is made easy by the human condition. The rite of Judaism turns a natural and common experience into the enactment and celebration of another place and time and world altogether. The words that change the public union of two private persons call upon encompassing eternity. With the wedding the change is from the here and the now to Eden past and Zion redeemed at the end of time, perfection to perfection.

The enchantment transforms the space, time, action, and community of the "I" of the groom and the "I" of the bride. The space is contained by the huppah which (done right) is constructed under the open sky— a contained space of heaven representing heaven. The time? It is now in the beginning. When else could it be? The action then invokes creation, the making of a new Eden. The community of the two "I"s becoming one "we" is the couple changed into the paradigm of humanity, beginning with Adam and Eve. Stripped down to essentials, the union of woman and man becomes the beginning of a new creation, so that the woman becomes Eve, the man, Adam. In this way is realized the prophecy of the snake in Eden, as the great medieval Bible interpreter, Rashi (1040–1105), explains matters. When the snake says, "... *but God knows that as soon as you eat of it, your eyes will be opened and you will be like God*" (Gen. 3:5), the meaning, Rashi maintains, is that you will become "creators of worlds." At the marriage rite a new world begins: a family, a social entity, humanity at the beginning of new creation of life.

That human experience of otherness, of being a bystander at a great event, in my memory is what turns the mere participant into an actor— someone who is two persons, the self and the self-made other. The groom dresses in costume, not in everyday clothes; he comes in procession, he does not merely walk; he stands center-stage, in a well-directed array of a cast. It is natural and right, therefore, that even as he sees himself as a witness to what is, in fact, happening to him, as actor in a play, so he should imagine the role he plays. The actors see themselves as separate from the role, while, with all great art, playing the role. That is why for them coming into a room is a reflected upon entrance. That duality of consciousness for us as actors too then opens a point of entry for the imagination.

It is for that reason that enchantment may take place, changing the natural moment into that something more that, in Judaism, we call holy. Turning to the marriage bower, we again ask: what are the roles being acted out by bride and groom in this odd drama? The specific words of enchantment answer that question, and there are two roles combined into one, two stages that blend. The first is the human being representing all humanity: man standing for Adam, woman for Eve. The second role, of course, is the humanity of Israel, the separate and sacred social entity, man and woman standing—through their joy on this unreservedly happy occasion—for Israel's joy, but also, therefore, for Israel's sorrow now and redemption then.

The enchantment works not one but many changes therefore in the new stage that is the marriage canopy, for each actor wears two masks, plays two parts—and maybe more. That map of many layers of translucent paper, each with its marking, shows the contours of the way only when all the sheets are in place. The man and wife become Adam and Eve in Eden, but also rejoicing Israel in the land redeemed. In that changed place and altered circumstance, time overflows the boundaries not only of the here and now but of then. Space is in more than one dimension, the action—as we shall see—is multiple, and the community is not only you and I, the "we" that takes shape, but that "we" that is all Israel, present at the beginning when an Israel takes shape.

That is what it means to say that the most intimate occasion, whether the birth of a child or the marriage ceremony, is also by its nature social, therefore public, communal, historical in a mythic sense. Here a new family begins. Individual lover and beloved celebrate the uniqueness, the privacy of their love. The nuptial prayer therefore cannot speak only of him and her, natural man and natural woman, as though the private life alone were celebrated, as if we come from nowhere and go nowhere and make no difference to anyone. The opposite is the truth. I come from a father and a mother and I become a parent; my life is with people; whatever I am and do is with people, that entity, Israel, conjured by Judaism out of a mass of individuals.

The rite comes to a climax in the Seven Blessings. But it unfolds in stages, beginning before the couple reaches the marriage canopy, ending long afterward. Seen in sequence, the rite follows this pattern: (1) *ketubah* is witnessed; (2) the bride's veil is put in place by the groom; (3) *erusin* under the *huppah*; (4) *nissuin* under the *huppah*. Walking through the rite, we come first to the touching moment when the groom places the veil over the bride's face, prior to the entry into the marriage canopy, and makes the following statement to her:

> May you, our sister, be fruitful and prosper. May God make you as Sarah, Rebecca, Rachel, and Leah. May the Lord bless you and keep you. May the Lord show you favor and be gracious to you. May the Lord show you kindness and grant you peace.[13]

The blessing of the groom for the bride invokes the matriarchs of Israel. We need not find this detail surprising. Rachel makes her appearance in the Seven Blessings, and as soon as we speak of Abraham, we think of Sarah, so too Isaac and Rebecca, Jacob and Leah and Rachel.

In focusing upon the drama, we should not lose sight of the occasion. The wedding takes place in the here and now, and in Judaism we do not lose sight of practical considerations. The bride is not only Eve, she is also a woman who bears responsibility to her husband. The groom, Adam, accepts responsibilities to and for his wife. The task of rite is not only to transform, but also to underline reality. In the case of the huppah, the rite of marriage, a legal transaction takes place, the formation of a social entity, a family, in which the rights and obligations of each party have to reach the expression and guarantee of a contract. In the case of the marriage ceremony, a marriage contract, called a ketubah, is signed and delivered from the groom to the bride's possession, and that takes place first in the order of the process. A précis of its contents follows:

> This ketubah witnesses before God and man that on the _____ day of the week, the _____ of the month _____, in the year 57__ __, the holy covenant of marriage was entered between bridegroom and his bride, at _____. Duly conscious of the solemn obligation of marriage the bridegroom made the following declaration to his bride: "Be consecrated to me as my wife according to the laws and traditions of Moses and Israel. I will love, honor and cherish you; I will protect and support you; and I will faithfully care for your needs, as prescribed by Jewish law and tradition." And the bride made the following declaration to the groom: "In accepting

the wedding ring I pledge you all my love and devotion and I take upon myself the fulfillment of all the duties incumbent upon a Jewish wife."

The Aramaic language of the ketubah specifies the legal standing of the husband's obligation to the wife. In order to pay what is owing to her, should he divorce her, or in order to provide for her if he dies before she does, the husband pledges even the shirt on his back. It is a serious occasion. Here is the counterpart to the blood of the circumcision. This part of the rite is commonly abbreviated in Conservative and Reform versions.

To understand the next stage in the rite—between the signing of witnesses on the ketubah and the recitation of the Seven Blessings, we have to call to mind the law of Judaism. That law knows a two-stage process by which a couple is united: one, *erusin,* in which the woman is sanctified, or designated as holy, to a particular man (betrothal), and the second, *nissuin*, in which the actual union is consecrated through the Seven Blessings. In ancient times these stages took place in an interval of as much as a full year. But today the wedding rite encompasses both. The first of the two is carried out under the marriage canopy by the drinking of a cup of wine with this blessing:

> Blessed are you, our God, king of the world, who create the fruit of the vine. Blessed are you, Lord our God, king of the world, who have sanctified us by your commandments and commanded us concerning proper sexual relations, forbidding to us betrothed women but permitting to us married women through the rites of the huppah and sanctification. Blessed are you, Lord, who sanctify your people Israel through the marriage canopy and the rite of sanctification.

Then there is a gift of a ring to the bride, with this formula:

> Behold you are sanctified to me by this ring in accord with the tradition of Moses and Israel.

That concludes the chapter of the rite known as erusin. Then come the Seven Blessings.

The climax of the rite of Adam and Eve, of man and wife as Israel in Jerusalem beyond time, comes in the recitation of Seven Blessings (*sheva berakhot*) over a cup of wine. At each appropriate turning, we ask about how the words invoke new worlds and call up from the deep a where, a when, and a who—which, although disembodied, are physically present. The following are those seven transforming statements of sanctification said over a cup of wine:

> 1. Praised are You, O Lord our God, King of the universe, creator of the fruit of the vine.

The rite takes its place over the cup of wine, the enchantment begins by turning the wine into something else than what it had been. Then comes the first action, invoking through words the world of Eden:

> 2. Praised are You, O Lord our God, King of the universe, who created all things for Your glory.
> 3. Praised are You, O Lord our God, King of the universe, creator of Adam.
> 4. Praised are You, O Lord our God, King of the universe, who created man and woman in Your image, fashioning woman from man as his mate, that together they might perpetuate life. Praised are You, O Lord, creator of man.

The sequence of three is perfectly realized: first, creation of all things, then, creation of man, then creation of man and woman in his image. These words invoke a world for which the occasion at hand serves as metaphor. "We now are like them then."

Israel's history begins with creation—first, the creation of the vine, a symbol of the natural world. Creation is for God's glory. All things speak to nature, to the physical as much as the spiritual, for all things were made by God. In Hebrew, the blessings end, "who formed the *Adam.*" All things glorify God; above all creation is Adam. The theme of ancient paradise is introduced by the simple choice of the word *Adam,* so heavy with meaning. The myth of man's creation is rehearsed: man and woman are in God's image, together complete and whole, creators of life, "like God." Woman was fashioned from man together with him to perpetuate life. And again, "blessed is the creator of Adam." We have moved, therefore, from the natural world to the archetypical realm of paradise. Before us we see not merely a man and a woman, but Adam and Eve.

The enchantment works its wonder by identifying the moment at hand, by telling us what we are like, that is, what is really happening. And under the circumstances formed by that mode of metaphorical thought, the reality that generates meaning is the out-there of "man and woman in his image," Eden, creation. The in-here—bride and groom wondering whether this is really true—then matches the out-there. The world is truly a stage, the men and women, really players. But here one actor takes two roles at once:

> 5. May Zion rejoice as her children are restored to her in joy. Praised are You, O Lord, who cause Zion to rejoice at her children's return.

A jarring intrusion, Zion comes uninvited. No one mentioned her. But given the standing of Zion as a metaphor for the resolution of Israel's exile and the human condition of suffering, simultaneously, who can find surprising the entry of this new character, this persona?

This Adam and this Eve also are Israel, children of Zion the mother, as expressed in the fifth blessing. Zion lies in ruins, her children scattered. Adam and Eve cannot celebrate together without thought to the condition of the mother, Jerusalem. The children will one day come home. The mood is hopeful yet sad, as it was meant to be, for archaic Israel mourns as it rejoices and rejoices as it mourns.

But lest mourning lead to melancholy, we return quickly to the happy occasion.

> 6. Grant perfect joy to these loving companions, as You did to the first man and woman in the Garden of Eden. Praised are You, O Lord, who grant the joy of bride and groom.

The joy of the moment gives a foretaste of the joy of restoration, redemption, return. Now the two roles become one in that same joy— first Adam and Eve (groom and bride), then Eden (the marriage canopy). That same joy comes, second, in the metaphors of Zion the bride and Israel the groom. But this is made very specific, for the words in italics allude to the vision of Jeremiah, when all seemed lost, that Jerusalem, about to fall and lose its people, will one day ring with the shouts of not the slaughtered and the enslaved but the returned and redeemed. That is why the concluding blessing returns to the theme of Jerusalem.

This time it evokes the tragic hour of Jerusalem's first destruction. When everyone had given up hope, supposing with the end of Jerusalem had come the end of time, only Jeremiah counseled renewed hope. With the enemy at the gate, he sang of coming gladness:

> Thus says the Lord: In this place of which you say, "It is a waste without human beings or animals," in the towns of Judah and the streets of Jerusalem that are desolate, without inhabitants, human or animal, *there shall once more be heard the voice of mirth and the voice of gladness, the voice of the bridegroom and the voice of the bride, the voices of those who sing as they bring thank offerings to the house of the Lord....*
> For I will restore the fortunes of the land as at first, says the Lord.
>
> *Jeremiah 33:10-11,* NRSV

The joy is not in two but in three masks: Eden then, marriage party now, and Zion in the coming age:

> 7. Praised are You, O Lord our God, King of the universe, who created joy and gladness, bride and groom, mirth, song, delight and rejoicing, love and harmony, peace and companionship. O Lord our God, may there ever *be heard in the cities of Judah and in the streets of Jerusalem voices of joy and gladness, voices of bride and groom, the jubilant voices of those joined in marriage under the bridal canopy, the voices of young people feasting and singing.*

The closing blessing is not merely a literary artifice or a learned allusion to the ancient prophet. It defines the exultant, jubilant climax of this acted-out myth: Just as here and now there stand before us Adam and Eve, so here and now in this wedding, the olden sorrow having been rehearsed, we listen to the voice of gladness that is coming. The joy of this new creation prefigures the joy of the Messiah's coming, hope for which is very present in this hour. And when he comes, the joy will echo the joy of bride and groom before us. Zion the bride, Israel the groom, united now as they will be reunited by the compassionate God— these stand under the marriage canopy.

But enchantment is just that. In the end, we are who we are: real man and real woman. And the bridal canopy, which stands for heaven and for Eden, is a prayer shawl stretched on four poles. Groom and bride rejoice not as metaphor but as fact. Then (in the received tradition) immediately leaving the canopy, they go to the bedroom (the first act of coition). In the innocent world in which sexual relations commence after the marriage—a rite known as *yihud*—solitary converse of bride and groom all by themselves for the first time is provided for, and to this the blessing refers:

> Praised are You, O Lord, who cause the groom to rejoice with his bride.

These seven blessings say nothing of private people and of their anonymously falling in love. Nor do they speak of the community of Israel, as one might expect on a public occasion. Lover and beloved rather are transformed from natural to mythical figures. The blessings speak of archetypical Israel, represented here and now by the bride and groom. All becomes credible not by what is said but by what is felt: that joy, that sense of witness to what we ourselves experience—these are the two ingredients that transform. The natural events of human life—here, the marriage of ordinary folk—are by myth heightened into a reenactment of Israel's life as a people. In marriage, individuals stand in the place of mythic figures, yet remain, after all, men and women. What gives their love its true meaning is their acting out the myth of creation, revelation, and redemption, here and now embodied in that love. But in the end, the sacred and secular are united in profane, physical love.

The wedding of symbol and everyday reality—the fusion and confusion of the two—these mark the classical Judaic enchantment that turns into a metaphor the natural and human sentiment, the joy of marriage. Invoking creation, Adam and Eve, the Garden of Eden, and the historical memory of the this-worldly destruction of an old, unexceptional temple, the private is turned public, the individual made into a paradigm. Ordinary events, such as a political and military defeat or success, are changed into theological categories such as divine punishment and heavenly compassion. If religion is a means of ultimate transformation, rendering the commonplace into the paradigmatic, changing the here and now into a moment of eternity and of eternal return, then the marriage liturgy serves to exemplify what is *religious* in Judaic existence. Time, space, action as these touch the passage of life lived one by one, the meal, the birth, the marriage—all are transformed through community, by which, we now realize, Judaism means the communion of the ages, the shared being of all who have lived in Israel and as Israel.

◇ —————————————————————————————————— ◇

Funerary Rites

The rites of death and burial are the final occasion of the life cycle. There is no evidence known to me on how many Jews are buried with Judaic—as distinct from nonsectarian or nonreligious—rites. My impression is that it is uncommon for Jews to be buried outside of Judaism. The ethnic loses hold, the religious takes over.

And that is not to be predicted by the character of the rites themselves—only by their social context, involving as they do home and family. Unlike the rites for circumcision and the marriage ceremony, funerary rites are few and general. Puberty and death, stages in the life cycle (for different reasons and in different ways), do not undergo that metamorphosis that turns a moment from what it merely seems to be into some other reality. In the Judaic transformation of the everyday, puberty and death remain pretty much untouched.

No metaphor from the corporate experience of Israel—no Elijah, no Adam and Eve, no slaves in Egypt—enchants the everyday. In death, it is I who die—not we. Nothing intervenes to turn the stark fact into something other than it is: the end of the life of an individual. No Moses, no Elijah, no David come to join the flights of angels that carry me to my rest. When I reach the age of responsibility for carrying out religious duties, I personally become responsible. No Phineas, no freed slaves join in celebration. I am changed, the occasion is not. And yet, most Judaists, when they die, are buried in the rites of Judaism (as well as many Jews who are not Judaists). The rites are very plain; there is no hiding death. The purpose and the fulfillment come when the corpse lies in the ground, and the religious duty is to pick up a shovel and pour dirt over the corpse. For that act of their children and grandchildren, the dead are grateful—no pretense here. The three moments of truth—circumcision with blood, marriage with a legal document, death with dirt on the corpse—even in popular Judaic practice these withstand contemporary taste for "spiritualization." The books prevail, but for a reason.

There is ample *halakhah* (norms of proper conduct, in a broad sense "law") for death. The importance of the rules for death and burial impresses people who otherwise observe little or nothing of the *halakhah*.

Why no rites at all for death and puberty? Because these are totally individual experiences. That is why there can be no appeal to "Israel," with its holy life, worldview. The radically isolated individual cannot be Israel. The reason is that the smallest whole unit of an Israel begins with family, that is, with a shared past. That is why birth undergoes the transformation of circumcision, which links the newborn to the increment of Israel. Marriage too is a family event, in which holy Israel has a stake in a way in which in death it does not. What makes the difference? Puberty marks no change in the makeup of the community, since the child enters the community at birth and never leaves. Puberty marks merely a shift in the status of an individual, who becomes responsible to the community and to its norms, to God and to God's will.

A review of the rites of death shows us that all things focus upon the individual, his or her condition, and, I claim, it is for that very reason that we invoke no transforming metaphor. At the onset of death, the dying Jew says a confession:

> My God and God of my fathers, accept my prayer. . . .
> Forgive me for all the sins which I have committed in my lifetime. . . .
> Accept my pain and suffering as atonement and forgive my wrong-doing,
>   for against You alone have I sinned. . . .
> I acknowledge that my life and recovery depend on You.
> May it be Your will to heal me.
> Yet if You have decreed that I shall die of this affliction,
> May my death atone for all sins and transgressions which I have committed
>   before You.
> Shelter me in the shadow of Your wings.
> Grant me a share in the world to come.
> Father of orphans and Guardian of widows, protect my beloved family. . . .
> Into Your hand I commit my soul. You redeem me, O Lord God of truth.
> Hear, O Israel, the Lord is our God, the Lord alone.
> The Lord He is God.
> The Lord He is God.

What is important in the confession in comparison to other critical rites of passage is its silence, for what the dying person does not invoke tells us more than what is said. To state matters very simply, excluding only the final three lines, there is not a word before us that cannot be said by any Gentile who believes in God, sin, atonement, judgment and reconciliation, which is to say, any Christian or Muslim. The concluding sentences identify the dying person with the holy community and its faith. But they too do not call to witness—to name familiar spirits— the slaves in Egypt, Adam and Eve, Elijah, or even the divine Judge seated before an open book and inscribing the fate of each person.

Nor do the books require a gesture to suggest otherwise. Everything that is done concerns the corpse, little invokes that transforming metaphor that makes of a meal a celebration of freedom; of having an out-of-door picnic a commemoration of Israel's wandering in the wilderness; a surgical operation a mark of eternal loyalty to God engraved in the flesh. The corpse is carefully washed and always protected. The body is covered in a white shroud, then laid in a coffin and buried. Normally burial takes place on the day of death or on the following day.

The burial rite at the graveside is laconic. The prayers that are said are exceedingly brief. One prayer that is commonly recited is as follows:

> The dust returns to the earth, as it was, but the spirit returns to God, who gave it. May the soul of the deceased be bound up in the bond of life eternal. Send comfort, O Lord, to those who mourn. Grant strength to those whose burden is sorrow.

It is common to intone the prayer *El Male Rahamim*, "O God, full of Compassion," the text of which is as follows:

> O God, full of compassion and exalted in the heights, grant perfect peace in your sheltering presence, among the holy and pure, to the soul of the deceased, who has gone to his eternal home. Master of mercy, we beseech you, remember all the worthy and righteous deeds that he performed in the land of the living. May his soul be bound up in the bond of life. The Lord is his portion. May he rest in peace. And let us say, Amen.[14]

The body is placed in the grave. Three pieces of broken pottery are laid on eyes and mouth as signs of their vanity. A handful of dirt from the Land of Israel is laid under the head.[15] The family recites the *ḳaddish,* an eschatological prayer of sanctification of God's name that looks forward to the messianic age and the resurrection of the dead. The prayer expresses the hope that the Messiah will soon come, "speedily, in our days," and that "he who brings harmony to the heavens will make peace on earth." The words of the Mourner's Kaddish exhibit the remarkable trait that they too remain silent, appealing to no metaphor, not even referring to death itself. The following is said in what was the vernacular when the prayer was composed, that is, Aramaic:

> May the great name [of God] be magnified and sanctified in the world which [God] created in accord with his will.
> And may his kingdom come in your life and days, and in the life of all the house of Israel, speedily, promptly.
> And say, Amen.

The community says:

> May the great name be blessed for ever and all eternity.

The mourner continues:

> May the holy name of the blessed one be blessed, praised, adored, exulted, raised up, adorned, raised high, praised,
> yet beyond all of those blessings, songs, praises, words of consolation, which we say in this world.
> And say, Amen.

The community says Amen.

> May great peace [descend] from heaven, [and] life for us and for all Israel.
> And say, Amen.

The community says Amen. Now the foregoing comes in Hebrew:

> He who makes peace in the heights will make peace for us and for all Israel.
> And say, Amen.

The community says Amen. The family of the deceased as well as the assembled then shovel dirt onto the body until the grave is filled. Then two lines are formed, leading away from the grave, and the mourners are given the following blessing: "May the Omnipresent comfort you among the other mourners of Zion and Jerusalem." The appeal to Zion and Jerusalem, of course, refers to the Temple of old, which people mourn until the coming restoration, thus a messianic and eschatological reference—the only one.

According to the books, the mourners remain at home for a period of seven days and continue to recite the memorial kaddish for eleven months. My impression of popular practice of what "good Jews" do does not conform with that rite. There is also the rite of "sitting shiva"— remaining at home for seven days in various positions of conventional mourning, receiving the consolation of guests, conducting thrice-daily worship services in the home, refraining from certain routine practices as a mark of mourning. An account of these rites would not tell us how people actually conduct themselves. We do not know how many people do, or do not, recite the memorial kaddish for the specified span of time; or once a week; or ever. We do not know how many families conduct receiving hours prior to the funeral itself—a wake—which the law of Judaism explicitly forbids (the mourner has only one concern prior to the burial—preparing for the burial), but the advertisements in the newspapers suggest the practice is not unknown. Nor do we know how many families observe seven days or three days or no days of home mourning after burial. So we cannot speculate here on why this, not that, since so far as I can locate current studies, there is not a single survey of Judaic burial rites in North America.[16]

The life cycle for the private individual is simple, but for the individual as part of Israel, God's holy people, it is rich, absorbing, and encompassing. Life is lived with God's people, in God's service. And yet, we discern no appeal to presences other than God's, no metamorphosis of death into something more. All things stand for other things, but death stands for itself. In the Judaism of private life and home, people who practice no other rite of book Judaism follow the rules of burial and mourning. Here no myth is invoked that separates the Jew from common humanity; the message of the liturgy is scarcely particular at all; nor does myth transform the here and now into a never-never land of Eve and Adam. What you see is what there is, and what you say matches what you see: the single most practiced rite of book Judaism, and probably the rite most thoroughly recast by the Judaism that is actually practiced. We know what the books say, but we are not now sure of what, exactly, we are seeing, or explaining.

The Judaism of Holocaust and Redemption

What It Is, Where It Governs

◇

Another self-evidently valid Judaism flourishes in North America, be-sides the Judaism that all "good Jews" agree defines the norm. We know it is different from the Judaists' Judaism, and we also know it is practiced, alongside the Judaists' Judaism, by nearly all Judaists, as well as by the generality of Jews who are not Judaists. The key figures come in the following form:

contributed to a Jewish charity in 1989	62%
contributed to UJA/Federation campaign in 1989	45%

Add to this list political action in behalf of the state of Israel (e.g., contributing to a lobby such as American-Israel Political Action Com-mittee [AIPAC], writing letters to members of Congress, voting for candidates who favor the state of Israel and against those who oppose it, and you have a set of actions not primary or not known in book Judaism, but very important for Judaists as much as for Jews. Since these activities not only define traits of "good Jews," and so enjoy such normative status as exists in Judaism in North America, they have to be seen as practical actions that express deeply held convictions and formative attitudes—rites of some kind. So we turn to the question of another Judaism, moving from the rites, rapidly considered, to the tale of transcendence that turns an action into a rite, and a story into a narrative bearing transcendent meaning.

So how do we know one Judaism from another, and, in this setting, how shall we tell one set of Judaists from another? We distinguish one Judaism from another by examining the myth, ritual, and symbolic structure of a Judaic system and comparing the results with the myth, ritual, and symbolic structure of another Judaic system. And we are not going to tell one set of Judaists from another, for we shall soon realize that each Judaism addresses a distinct range of social experience. The Judaism that emerges from the holy books predominates at home and in the family, reshaping life cycle events; the other Judaism addresses the experience of people not at home or in private but in their lives together and in community. The one Judaism, with its rituals and transcendent tale, explains one component of the social world; the other, a different component of that same social world, and the same Judaists who worship on the Day of Atonement but not on the Sabbath are the ones who support the state of Israel but (as we shall observe in chapter 7) do not go to live there. In each case, "good Jews" know how to pick and choose.¹ But each of the two Judaisms serves in its place, to make sense of its assigned realm of human experience, the private and the public, respectively.

In North America, a second Judaic system flourishes alongside the Judaism of the dual Torah and is practiced by the same Judaists. The Judaism of the dual Torah appeals to the myth that at Sinai God revealed the Torah to Moses in two media: written (Scripture as we know it) and oral (ultimately written down in the Mishnah, Talmuds, Midrash, and related documents). Its ritual involves the rites we have examined and others we shall consider in chapter 7); its symbolic structure rests on the symbol of the Torah, the centerpiece of worship and discourse. The correlative Judaism is the Judaism of Holocaust and Redemption, which has translated the catastrophe of European Jewry from 1933 through 1945 and the founding of the Jewish state in Palestine as the state of Israel in 1948 and the state's successful history from then on into events of transcendent proportions and cosmic meaning: murder become Holocaust, and the consequent creation of the state of Israel, Redemption.

The ritual of that other Judaism involves political action and enormous communal organization and activity. Its counterpart to the Day of Atonement is the fund-raising dinner of the local Jewish Federation and Welfare Fund and United Jewish Appeal campaign for the state of Israel and other Jewish causes. Its counterpart to the bar or bat mitzvah is a summer vacation in the state of Israel. Its equivalent to the intense moments of marriage and death is the pilgrimage to Auschwitz followed by a flight to Jerusalem and procession to the Western Wall in Jerusalem. Its places of worship comprise Holocaust museums, and its moments of celebration include commemorations of the Holocaust on a day set aside for that purpose. Its "study of the Torah" involves visits to Holocaust museums and courses on the German war against the Jews and the death factories of Europe. Its memorial of the destruction of the Temple finds expression in recitations of how the Germans massacred Jews by firing squads, by asphyxiation, and by driving them into a barn and setting it on fire. These things really happened, of course, but long ago and far away, just as Sinai really happened. But recovered by memory, they live and inform, just as much as Sinai is constantly remembered in the Torah, in the covenant.

The power of the Judaism of Holocaust and Redemption differs not at all in its appeal to facts reconstituted in vivid imagination—that is, the power of memory; but the memories are different. Memory, as I have argued in prior chapters, is evoked by rite when social experience corresponds to the message of the rite. The received tradition remains inert when nothing in our experience makes its message plausible. In the case of the Judaism of Holocaust and Redemption, the experience to which it appeals for plausibility is immediate, and it accurately replicates, in the language of history, a felt social experience of Jews in North America: their sense that difference far from defining destiny shades over into disability and discrimination. Holocaust states in extreme form what Gentiles are capable of doing and have done to Jews. And Redemption provides the remission of the horror of history.

Why is it that the Judaism of the books, that is, the Judaism of the dual Torah, finds a firm position in the shared imagination of Judaists in one part of the social order—the familial and personal and private—while the Judaism of Holocaust and Redemption occupies the center of the social order that is public, corporate, and communal? I have stressed that those rites of book Judaism that form important components of the North American Judaists' Judaism focus on home and family. As we shall see in chapter 7, there are other rites of that same book

Judaism that are nearly universally dismissed as utterly implausible by those same Judaists, and all of those rites lay heavy emphasis not upon individual and family life, but on the life of the corporate community— holy Israel.

If that fact exhaustively characterized the life of Judaists (and other Jews as well), we should plausibly conclude, then, that "Judaism" has been privatized, and the life of the faith reduced to the dimensions only of home and family. But the facts prove otherwise. Judaic public behavior extends to what is communal, public, and corporate: "contribute to Jewish charity," "give to UJA." Judaists also are activists in Jewry when shared and public action of a political character is demanded of "all good Jews." The consensus of Judaists focuses upon corporate as much as private dimensions of the social order. The fact is the opposite, namely, that a distinct Judaism—one that answers another sort of questions altogether—has taken shape and, in fact, has entered the center of public life and activity, taking the place of those elements of the program of public life and activity set forth by the received, book Judaism.

So the appearance of indifference to the corporate dimensions of the holy life of book Judaism (which we shall examine in chapter 7) should not deceive us. Not only do Jews form a corporate community and share a substantial range of social experience; that shared public life itself takes shape in response to a Judaism and forms a religious system. But, as I said, it is not the same Judaism, the same religious system, that governs in private life. The reason is that this other Judaism answers the urgent questions that the community at large asks itself, and, it follows, its answers are found self-evidently true, therefore its rites predominate, and other rites for the community fall by the way. When we know the answers, we may then form the questions, comparing the questions to the social world of those who ask those questions with urgency.

That shared social experience in politics also takes form in transformations of the given into a gift, so that the "is" of the everyday polity shades into the "as if" of another time and place, as much as is the case in the transformation by the Judaism of the dual Torah of the passage of the individual through the cycle of life. We shall now see that American and Canadian Jews in politics as much as in private life see themselves in the model of an imagined paradigm, one in substance different from, but in structure the same as, the Passover seder, that is,

"as if they were liberated." Jews conduct public business, with remarkable unanimity, as though they were somewhere else and someone
else than where and what they are. Specifically, in politics, history, in
society, even in economics, Jews in North America may not only point
to shared traits and experiences but also claim to exhibit a viewpoint
in common that leads to readily discerned patterns of belief and behavior.

Let us begin by showing that Jews do form a community beyond
the family and home, so that we may appeal to a shared public experience,
a polity in common, in our call for an everyday to be changed into
another world. Those indicative traits that point toward social continuity
and corporate cohesion in point of fact encompass social processes such
as marriage and family formation, residence and mobility, social class,
occupation, education, economic status, communal affiliation and identification and behavior. Family, stratification of Jewish society, and diverse characteristics of ethnicity—all define indicators to mark the Jews
as a group distinctive in their larger social setting. As Calvin Goldscheider says:

> There are critical links between family and stratification, between
> social class and migration, between jobs, residence, education, family, and
> ethnicity.[2]

Goldscheider's and others' studies have shown that the Jews do form
a distinctive social group, with the indicators of difference sharply etched
and well framed:

> A detailed examination of family, marriage, childbearing, social class, res-
> idence, occupation and education among Jews and non-Jews leads to the
> unmistakable conclusion that Jews are different. Their distinctiveness as a
> community is further reinforced by religious and ethnic forms of cohe-
> siveness. . . . Jewish exceptionalism means more than the absence of assim-
> ilation. The distinctive features of American Jewish life imply bonds and
> linkages among Jews which form the multiple bases of communal conti-
> nuity. These ties are structural as well as cultural; they reflect deeply
> embedded forms of family, educational, job and residence patterns, rein-
> forced by religious and ethnic-communal behavior, cemented by shared
> lifestyles and values.[3]

So much for the fact that Jews in the United States and Canada constitute
a profoundly united and amply differentiated community. A broad range

of indicators point toward the boundaries that distinguish Jewry from other groups. There is a shared corporate experience of polity, and that is distinctive to Jewry at large and transcends genealogy, on the one side, and individual taste and judgment and belief, on the other.

Not only so, American and Canadian Jews do share a transforming perspective, which imparts to their public as much as to their private vision a different set of spectacles from those worn by everybody else in the sheltering society of America or Canada. There is not only a Jewish-ethnic, but a Judaic-religious corporate experience in public life, and, while it does not self-evidently lead to the synagogue, it does enchant vision and change perspective and persons. There are cosmic narratives and rites to which people do respond, even though they are not those of the received Judaism. And the Judaic system that takes the place of the received Judaism in the life of the community at large indeed occupies its share of the place reserved for the unique, the self-evident truths beyond argument.

What is this other Judaism—the Judaism of Holocaust and Redemption? Let me spell out the worldview and way of life of a Judaism that exercises the power to transform civic and public affairs in Jewry as much as the Judaism of the dual Torah enchants and changes the personal and familial ones. In politics, history, and society, Jews in North America respond to the Judaism of the Holocaust and Redemption in such a way as to imagine they are someone else, living somewhere else, at another time and circumstance. That vision transforms families into an Israel, a community. The somewhere else is Poland in 1944 and the earthly Jerusalem, and the vision turns them from reasonably secure citizens of America or Canada into insecure refugees finding hope and life in the state of Israel. Public events commemorate, so that "we" were there in "Auschwitz," which stands for all of the centers for the murder of Jews, and "we" share, too, in the everyday life of that faraway place in which we do not live but should, the state of Israel. That transformation of time and of place, no less than the recasting accomplished by the Passover seder or the rite of berit milah or the huppah, turns people into something other than what they are in the here and now.

The issues of this public Judaism, the civil religion of North American Jewry (and not theirs alone), are perceived to be political. That means, the questions to which this Judaism provides answers are raised by peoples' public and social experience, not the experience of home and family and the passage through life from birth to death. But the power of that Judaism to turn things into something other than what they seem, to teach lessons that change the everyday into the remarkable—that power works no less wonderfully than does the power of the other Judaism to change me into Adam or one of the Israelites that crossed the Red Sea.

The lessons of the two Judaisms, of course, are not the same. The Judaism of the dual Torah teaches about the sanctification of the everyday in the road toward the salvation of the holy people. The Judaism of Holocaust and Redemption tells me that the everyday—the here and the now of home and family—ends not in a new Eden but in a cloud of gas; that salvation comes today if I will it, but not here and not now. And it teaches me not to trouble to sanctify, and also not even to trust the present circumstance.

The transcendent message[4] of the Judaism of Holocaust and Redemption comes to expression in the words of the great theologian Emil Fackenheim who maintains that "the Holocaust" has produced an eleventh commandment, "Not to hand Hitler any more victories." The commanding voice of Sinai gave Ten Commandments, the commanding voice of Auschwitz, the eleventh. The Ten call for us to become like God in the ways in which the image of God may be graven, which is, by keeping the Sabbath and honoring the other and having no other gods but God. The eleventh tells us what we must not do; it appeals not to love God but to spite a man. So does politics transform. The Judaism of Holocaust and Redemption supplies the words that make another world of this one. Those words, moreover, change the assembly of like-minded individuals into occasions for the celebration of the group and the commemoration of its shared memories.

Not only so, but events defined, meetings called, moments identified as distinctive and holy by that Judaism of Holocaust and Redemption mark the public calendar and draw people from home and family to collectivity and community instead of the occasions of the sacred calendar of the synagogue—that is, the life of Israel as defined by the Torah. In the United States religions address the realm of individuals and families, but a civil religion defines public discourse on matters of value and ultimate concern. The Judaism of the dual Torah forms the counterpart

to Christianity, and the Judaism of Holocaust and Redemption constitutes Jewry's civil religion.

I have spoken of the social experience that imparts plausibility to
one rite of Judaism but not to some other aspect of that same Judaism—
the Passover seder, for example. It remains to ask, what social experience
makes not only plausible but urgent and self-evidently true (thus, relevant) the Judaism of Holocaust and Redemption? From the tale that
it tells, we may identify the social experience of the living generation
to which people refer when hearing that tale, the aspect of self-evidence.
Now I shall define in detail the rites and activities of this other and
competing Judaism, the story that it tells corresponding to slaves' escaping from Egypt or Adam and Eve under the huppah; and I shall
explain its political program. Only then will we be able to assess the
impact, upon the received Judaism, of the civil religion of Holocaust
and Redemption.

"The Holocaust" of the Judaism of Holocaust and Redemption refers
to the murder of six million Jewish children, women, and men in Europe
between 1933 and 1945 by the Germans. "The Redemption" is the
creation of the state of Israel. Both events constitute essentially political
happenings; a government was responsible for the one, a state and
government emerged from the other. And both events involved collectivities acting in the realm of public policy. The Holocaust then corresponds in the here and now to anti-Semitism, exclusion, alienation,
which Jews experience solely by reason of being Jewish. And, while
authentic anti-Semitism—hatred of Jews as the cause of all evil; loathing
of Judaism as a wicked religion; pointing to Jews as the source of every
disaster—flourishes only on the lunatic fringe of politics, and in certain
circles of racist ideologues, the experience of difference is a commonplace
and routine experience for North American Jews—and that is by definition! The one shared, public, corporate, communal experience all
Jews have is that they are different from Gentiles. The Judaism of the
dual Torah explains that difference as destiny and invokes the covenant
to explain it, the category of sanctification to justify it. The Judaism of
Holocaust and Redemption explains that difference differently. But
while only some Jews find a correspondence between covenant and
imagined status as God's holy people, all Jews see themselves on a
continuum with the Holocaust: if I had been there, I too would have
been gassed and cremated.

To state this Judaism in a few words: the worldview of the Judaism of Holocaust and Redemption stresses the unique character of the murders of European Jews, the providential and redemptive meaning of the creation of the state of Israel. The way of life of this Judaism requires active work in raising money and political support for the state of Israel. Different from Zionism, which held that Jews should live in a Jewish state, this system serves, in particular, to give Jews living in America a reason and an explanation for being Jewish. This Judaism therefore lays particular stress on the complementarity of the political experiences of mid-twentieth-century Jewry: the mass murder in death factories of six million European Jews, and the creation of the state of Israel three years after the end of the massacre. The system as a whole presents an encompassing transcendent message, linking one event to the other as an instructive pattern, and moves Jews to follow a particular set of actions as it tells them why they should be Jewish. In short, the civil religion of Jewry addresses issues of definition of the group and the policies it should follow to sustain its ongoing life and protect its integrity.

That explains how the Judaism of Holocaust and Redemption affirms and explains in this-worldly terms the Jews' distinctiveness. When did this Judaism come to the fore? It forms, within Jewry, a chapter in a larger movement of ethnic assertion in America. Attaining popularity in the late 1960s, the Judaism of Holocaust and Redemption came to the surface at the same time that black assertion, Italo-American and Polish-American affirmation, and feminist movements attained prominence. That movement of rediscovery of difference responded to the completion of the work of assimilation to American civilization and its norms.

Once people spoke English without a foreign accent, they could once more think about learning Polish or Yiddish or Norwegian. It then became safe and charming. Just as when black students demanded what they deemed ethnically characteristic food, so Jewish students discovered they wanted kosher food too. In that context the Judaism of Holocaust and Redemption came into sharp focus, with its answers to unavoidable questions deemed to relate to public policy: Who are we? Why should we be Jewish? What does it mean to be Jewish? How do we relate to Jews in other times and places? What does the state of Israel mean to us, and what are we to it? Who are we in American society? These and other questions form the agenda for the Judaism of Holocaust and Redemption.

The power of the Judaism of the Holocaust and Redemption to frame Jews' public policy—to the near-exclusion of the Judaism of the dual Torah—may be shown very simply. The Holocaust formed the question; redemption in the form of the creation of the state of Israel, the answer, for all universally appealing Jewish public activity and discourse. Synagogues (except for specified occasions) appeal to a few, but activities that express the competing Judaism appeal to nearly everybody. That is to say, nearly all American Jews identify with the state of Israel and regard its welfare not only as a secular good, but a metaphysical necessity. Nearly all American Jews are supporters of the state of Israel. But they also regard their own "being Jewish" as inextricably bound up with the meaning they impute to the Jewish state.[5] In many ways these Jews relive every day of their lives the terror-filled years during which European Jews were wiped out—and every day they do something about it.

It is as if people spent their lives trying to live out a cosmic myth and, through rites of expiation and regeneration, accomplished the goal of purification and renewal. Access to the life of feeling and experience—to the way of life that made one distinctive without leaving the person terribly different from everybody else—emerged in the Judaic system of Holocaust and Redemption. The Judaism of Holocaust and Redemption presents an immediately accessible message, cast in extreme emotions of terror and triumph, its round of endless activity demanding only spare time. That Judaism realizes in a poignant way the conflicting demands of Jewish Americans to be intensely Jewish, but only once in a while, providing a means of expressing difference in public and in politics while not exacting much of a cost in meaningful everyday difference from others.

At issue, therefore, is not whether Jews see and do things together. They do. At issue is whether or not they do *religious* things together, and, as we have seen, still more concretely why they share or appeal and respond to some, but not other, religious things. The realm of the sacred touches their passage through life and draws them into contact with others principally through home and family. What people do together and share also passes under the transforming power of imagination. What they do not share is not subject to that metamorphosis of vision that changes the "is" into the "what if." In the religious life of Judaism, everything that works its wonder for the generality of Jews proves personal and familial, not communal—and that despite the remarkable facts of Jewish distinctiveness within the larger society of America and Canada. The social experience forms the premise of the religious life.

But the Jews' social experience of polity and community does not match the religious experience of home and family. Hence the religious side to things conforms to the boundaries of family, and the public experience of politics, economics, and society that Jews share comes to expression in quite different ways altogether. I see two fundamental reasons for the present state of affairs, which finds Judaism intensely affective in the private life and remarkably irrelevant to the public. The one is the prevailing attitude toward religion and its correct realm; the other is the Jews' reading of their experience of the twentieth century, which has defined as the paramount mode of interpreting social experience a paradigm other than that deriving from Israel as the holy people. Let me explain what I mean by the first of the two, the definition of the proper place of religion in public and political life.[6]

These two Judaisms—that of the dual Torah, that of Holocaust and Redemption—flourish side by side, the one viewed as self-evidently valid at home, the other taken to be obvious and beyond all need of proof or demonstration in the public discourse. The words that evoke worlds that transform for the community—that reach public and socially shared emotions and turn occasions into events, in the Jews' life—speak as a group, just as the liturgy of the synagogue speaks of murder and survival. The topic now is public policy, politics, how we should relate to the world beyond. And, in the nature of public life in North America, that topic is taken to be not other-worldly and supernatural (*Adam and Eve in Eden*), but this-worldly and political, involving the affairs of nations and states. The received Judaism of the dual Torah, with its Adam and Eve, Abraham, Isaac, and Jacob, slaves in Egypt, Moses on Sinai, sanctification in the here and now and salvation at the end of time—that Judaism exercises power at home. But it does not, nor is it understood to, pertain to the issues of public policy and politics that Jewry, as a collectivity, chooses to address. That other Judaism, which speaks of history and politics, things that have really happened and their implications in the here and now, takes over when the Jew leaves home.

If, as we have seen, the received Judaism thrives in the private life of home and family, where, in general, religion in North America is understood to work its wonders, that other Judaism makes its way in the public arena, where, in general, politics and public policy, viewed as distinct from religion, function. The Judaism of Holocaust and Redemption is political in its themes and character, cosmic truth and rites. The worldview of the Judaism of Holocaust and Redemption evokes political, historical events—the destruction of the Jews in Europe and the creation of the state of Israel, two events of a wholly political character. It treats these events as unique, just as the Judaism of the dual Torah treats Eden and Adam's fall, Sinai, and the coming redemption, as unique. It finds in these events the ultimate meaning of the life of the Jews together as Israel and it therefore defines an Israel for itself—the state of Israel—just as the Judaism of the dual Torah finds in Eden, Sinai, and the world to come the meaning of the life of Israel and so defines for itself an Israel too—the holy Israel, the social entity different in its very essence from all other social entities. The Judaism of Holocaust and Redemption addresses the issues of politics and public policy that Jews take up in their collective social activity.

So much for the "this" of "why this, not that." Now let us turn to the "that"—things that fall well beyond the limits of plausibility in the Judaism of the Judaists of North America.

PART III

WHY NOT THAT?

CHAPTER 7

What Most Judaists
Ignore—and Why

◇

The catalogue of rites and myths North American Jews neglect or
dismiss exceeds—and also in anomalous ways simply differs from—
the list of beliefs and practices that, for Judaists, define "a good Jew."
That single sentence could easily suffice to state the message of this
chapter, if the conventional agenda sufficed. But at stake is not a list
but a principle of differentiation, and, for that purpose, we require both
a generalization and an example thereof. The form of the generalization
will present no surprise, since I have insisted upon it time and again.

First, Judaists identify with the experiences of the individual that
are plausibly transformed in rites of passage and events in the home
and family into encounters with transcendence.[1] That is why the social
imagination of Jewry engages with Judaism in its narrative of the rites
of the passage through life, on the one side, and of a social experience
mediating between home and family and the sheltering world, on the
other. Circumcision and the Passover seder bear in common a single
social referent: family, home, and experiences of essentially private life.
The theological message of the rites corresponds to the social experience
of the faithful who practice those rites.[2]

Second, rites that focus on community and public affairs, by contrast,
fail because they invoke in common another social referent: society
beyond individual and family. So there is one set of social experiences

123

that correspond to the myth and ritual of individual, home, and family; there is another set of social experiences that correspond to the transcendent tale and ritual of corporate Jewry—Israel all together. And they do not seem to match, intersecting in many people to be sure, but hardly corresponding in the essentials of symbol, myth, and ritual.

Why does the Judaism of the dual Torah work where it works but not work in other areas? Because its message fits some areas but not others, and people know the difference. What is that difference and how do people know the difference, so that they confidently define "a good Jew"? I stated at the outset that I think religious beliefs, attitudes, sentiments and emotions matter a great deal—pro and also con. Emotions and opinions, attitudes and propositions, respond to the perceived social reality that people know as the datum of their life. So, in my view, where the Judaism of the dual Torah invokes the myth of covenant and commandment, it contradicts the social experience of the life lived in privacy, the singularity of home and family.

That Judaism does not serve, but one that more accurately corresponds to the experienced world does. The Judaism of the dual Torah speaks plausibly of what is shared, and is silent about what is not shared. The rites of that Judaism that bear deep meaning speak of resentment against a social order and of freedom, or of Adam and Eve in Eden. The rites of the Judaism of Holocaust and Redemption that attain the compelling force of self-evidence speak of resentment and fear, the shared experience of an uncomfortable minority. That is what the successes of the two Judaisms have in common—that, and one other thing. Neither speaks of "must" but only "may," both Judaisms preserve freedom to choose, and concerning covenant and obligation and the God who commands and the Israel that obeys, neither Judaism (as shaped by the people out there, not the books in here) says anything. From what the two Judaisms say, as much as from what they do not say, we hear the message: this is plausible, that is not; good Jews do this but don't have to do (or believe) that.

Specifically, what is personal and private imposes no discipline, no objective obligation. What I do at home, I do because I want to. What I do in the synagogue, in public, I do in response to norms I cannot, on my own, shape. The difference between why this? and why not that? takes shape at the dividing point between the optional and the obligatory, or, in the language of Judaism, on the frontier of the norm for behavior—halakhah. To state matters simply, Why this? Because I want to. Why not that? Because (if that) I have to. Mordecai M. Kaplan, the founder of Reconstructionist Judaism, stated forthrightly: "mitzvot yes, averot no," meaning, yes to religious duty, no to religiously defined transgression; and if there is no obligation, there can be no transgression.

The "why not" then stands not merely for a no to what is public and communal; after all, we have dwelt on the public and communal Judaism of Holocaust and Redemption. The two Judaisms that the people have shaped for themselves cohabit because they make a single statement; they part company only at the point at which their statements resonate. The statement both make underlines not only resentment but also the possibility of resistance: "we" can make it in this society no matter what they do to us (Hanukkah, Passover). These are messages that speak for both Jews and Judaists. They are messages of courage and humanity (which I respect, since I share the certainty of self-evidence that I try also to describe and analyze and interpret).

But courage and humanity are messages that the books cannot deliver but dismiss. The people so act as to subvert the center of the books, the message of covenant made with a zealous, commanding God, who so loves Israel as to care even what they eat for breakfast and when they have sexual relations. Andrew Greeley's stunning metaphor of "God as a teen-age lover" captures the urgency of the holy books. The one point on which both Judaisms differ forms the main point of the books. It is also what characterizes and differentiates what the people do.

The "why not" then rejects what is obligatory or subject to public regulation. The premise of what the people do is that religion is a matter of one's own choice—hence the centrality of home and family, rites of passage and subjective liturgy. And the Judaism of Holocaust and Redemption depends upon the willing obedience of the faithful—obedience given by choice or withheld by one's own will, as much as the Judaism of rites of passage and celebration at home depends upon options taken. Fackenheim's "commanding voice of Auschwitz," which approaches the borders of covenant and commandment, bears a negative message from a place of evil without end. So the differentiating criterion that tells people what they need not do is very simple: "you don't have to . . . ," and there follows whatever comes to mind. And there is no "you do have to" to which all "good Jews" respond, except because they feel like it (for reasons I have stressed in earlier chapters).

What is it in the experience of the social order that renders the "ought" of the Torah's commandments implausible, therefore irrelevant? In Jewry (and not there alone) people experience a cogent social world, one of integrity and inner coherence, beginning and ending with family. Society beyond presents diversities, both within Jewry and beyond, such that people cannot refer to a cogent religious life (so far as they define religion as personal, not political) beyond family. It is simply not there. Quite to the contrary, the plurality of society in general and the diversity of Jewry in particular prevent the formation of that sense of corporate existence beyond the individual in family that would lay foundations for a shared experience of transformation, through rites' enchantment, of the given into a gift. As we shall presently notice, to be sure, there is a corporate experience of being Israel, and it does yield a cogent system of a wholly political and public character.

But that system differs from this and affects another mode of existence than the one perceived to be personal, familial, religious. When I observed in chapter 1 that the point of departure between what the books say and what the people do emerges at the deepest layers of premise, that is what I meant: the holy books presuppose a holy people, living apart, and also experiencing an entirely cogent social world: Jews living mainly with other Jews, eating Jewish food, talking a Jewish language, wearing Jewish clothes, engaged in Jewish occupations, studying Jewish books, living wholly Jewish lives. But the people do not talk, eat, think, sleep, and live "Jewish." That is the parting of the paths, and that has made all the difference. People who have no experience of a coherent society and who do not hanker after a corporate community do their best with what they have: the life they live, the books they read.

It follows that, within the nurture of the Jewish life, the experience of reality ends with the family. Whatever is beyond is an "as if." The encounter with reality in the undifferentiated society ends with job and home. The community—other than the city in which we live—is an "out there." Then we wonder what in the received social experience of the Jewish people is supposed to define the condition of the holy Israel, sharing a corporate sacral existence defined by God's rules. The answer to that question leads us from description of the here and now to an account of the world of "ought" formed out of the holy books. For I cannot direct the reader's attention to a present world of Judaism in which, for an entire encompassing society, the enchantment transforms polity as well as family—a society or community out there in its entirety. Neighborhoods or villages yes, but these form ghettos, made by decision of people to manufacture a society through self-segregation. When the families of Israel formed, in the aggregate, the corporate and cogent society of all Israel, it was not by choice but by the nature of the polity itself. Jews saw a commonality beyond themselves. They did not think they invented it but knew that God had decreed it. Today when communities take shape, it is because families decide. The community grows by incremental decision, not by divine decree. Growing up in a Reform Temple in West Hartford, Connecticut, I remember incessant and unresolved Youth Group discussions on, "why should I be Jewish?" It never occurred to me, as a preteen-ager right in the middle of the Holocaust, that I had no choice.

So to the main "not that," formed by the norms, of whatever character or definition. Halakhah—the norm for conduct, whether ethical or ritual, private or public—defines. It governs whether or not people want it to. That is, the norms of the group come before the individual or family in the definition of the way of life, and the individual or family does not make decisions except within the consensus of the community formed, from of old, in the halakhah. The community—nation, people, society, however the social entity be called—transcends the individual and the family, coming before and continuing afterward, and it is the community that dictates the circumstance of enchantment and transformation, lending credibility to what, when done on an individual basis only, is mere magic.

Accordingly, rules shared in common turn individuals and families into a community. Then, but only then, the enchantment of rite transforms the shared experience of the community, asking questions urgent not to the individual or family primarily, but to the community first of all—questions of culture and value, of work and leisure. Second, the group expresses its sense of self in a worldview formed on a shared imagination, *as if* it were held in common. For the *as if* becomes the *is* only when enough people join in the drama, when the audience is on stage, so to speak.

Short of community, a vision of a community held only by radically isolated individuals or mere aggregates of families frames the perspective of the sect or the commune or the ghetto. All three have in common the defining of the self against the other, a reliance on the outsider to lend credibility to the sect's or commune's or ghetto's isolation and fantasy of isolation. With these matters clear, we ask ourselves how, in the circumstance of a corporate society, Judaism spelled out the world-view and the way of life in which the corporate, not only the private rites worked their magic.

So, as is clear, the way of life of corporate, holy Israel finds definition in halakhah, by which people state (after the fact mostly) those rules that describe the life they lead. In halakhah they record the actions that turn one thing into something else, the sexual union of man and woman into a contracted relationship sanctified by Heaven, for example; the preparation of food into the consecration of the meal; or the saying of words into prayer. Halakhah therefore constitutes the way of life that, prior to and beyond the experience of family, forms of families a corporate, holy community, Israel in God's sight. When people think of law, they ordinarily imagine a religion for bookkeepers who tote up the good deeds and debit the bad and call the result salvation or damnation, depending on the outcome.

But when we speak of life under halakhah we mean life obligatorily conducted in accord with the compulsory—the rules and regulations of the holy life. The mythic structure built upon the themes of creation, revelation, and redemption finds expression, not only in synagogue liturgy, but especially in concrete, everyday actions or action-symbols— that is, deeds that embody and express the fundamental mythic life of the classical Judaic tradition. So far as the formula or incantation is carried by the blessing or prayer, the gesture of enchantment takes form in halakhah. Judaism transforms the ordinary into the holy through both, and the rite on the remarkable occasion takes second place behind the ritualization of the everyday and commonplace, that is to say, the sanctification of the ordinary.

The word halakhah is normally translated "law," for the halakhah is full of normative, prescriptive rules about what one must do and refrain from doing in every situation of life and at every moment of the day. But halakhah derives from the root *halakh,* "go," and a better translation would be "way." The halakhah is *the way* we live life; *the way* we shape the daily routine into a pattern of sanctity; *the way* we follow the revelation of the Torah and attain redemption. For the Judaic religious encounter, this *way* is absolutely central. Belief without the expression of belief in the workaday world is of limited consequence. To refer to the enchanted world beyond and within the faith or the Torah, the purpose of revelation is to create a kingdom of priests and a holy people. The foundation of that kingdom, or sovereignty, is the rule of God over the lives of humanity. For the Judaic tradition, God rules much as people do, by guiding others on the path of life, not by removing them from the land of living. Creation lies behind; redemption, in the future; Torah is for here and now. To the classical Jew, Torah means revealed law or commandment, accepted by Israel and obeyed from Sinai to the end of days.

Within the norms inhere messages as engaging as the messages of the seder or the huppah. For we are not talking about logic-chopping, nit-picking, obsessive-compulsive behavior, a kind of religious behaviorism of robots under the law. We address an ennobling and purifying theory of what it means to be human, "in our image, after our likeness." To understand what it means in Judaism to be a human being in God's image, after God's likeness, we turn to the halakhah's theory of humanity, the anthropology of Judaism. And what is it that we may expect to find? The spirit of the Jewish way (halakhah) is conveyed in many modes, for law is not divorced from values, but rather concretizes human beliefs and ideals. The purpose of the commandments is to show the road to sanctity, the way to God. In a more mundane sense, the following provides a valuable insight:

> Rava [a fourth-century rabbi] said, "When a person is brought in for judgment in the world to come, that person is asked, 'Did you deal in good faith? Did you set aside time for study of Torah? Did you engage in procreation? Did you look forward to salvation? Did you engage in the dialectics of wisdom? Did you look deeply into matters?' "
>
> Babylonian Talmud, Shabbat, 31a

Rava's interpretation of Isa. 33:6, *and there shall be faith in thy times, strength, salvation, wisdom and knowledge*, provides one glimpse into the life of the Jew who followed the way of Torah. The first consideration was ethical: Did the Jew conduct affairs faithfully? The second was study of Torah, not at random but every day, systematically, as a discipline of life. Third came the raising of a family, for celibacy and abstinence from sexual life were regarded as sinful; the full use of woman's and man's creative powers for the procreation of life was a commandment. Nothing God made was evil. Wholesome conjugal life was a blessing. Fourth, merely living day-by-day according to an upright ethic was not sufficient. It is true that people must live by a holy discipline, but the discipline itself was only a means. The end was salvation. Hence the pious were asked to look forward to salvation, aiming their deed and directing their hearts toward a higher goal. Wisdom and insight—these completed the list, for without them, the way of Torah was a life of mere routine, rather than a constant search for deeper understanding.

The halakhah in detail meant to make a main point, and the literature of the halakhah, beginning with the Talmud, expressed that point quite articulately. One formulation of the entire Torah—law and theology alike—is attributed to Hillel, a first-century authority:

> What is hateful to yourself do not do to your fellow-man. That is the whole Torah. All the rest is commentary. Now go and study.
>
> Babylonian Talmud, Shabbat, 31a

The saying assigned to Hillel was neither the first nor the last to provide a pithy definition of the Torah or Judaism. In his definition we see that from among many available verses of Scripture the selected model is Lev. 19:18: *You shall love your neighbor as yourself: I am the Lord.* This commandment summarized everything. Still a further definition of the purpose of the halakhah as it defines the religious duties, or commandments incumbent on all Jews as corporate Israel, derives from later rabbis of the Talmud. Simlai expounded:

> Six hundred and thirteen commandments were given to Moses, three hundred and sixty-five negative ones, corresponding to the number of the days of the solar year, and two hundred forty-eight positive commandments, corresponding to the parts of man's body.
>   David came and reduced them to eleven: *A Psalm of David* [Psalm 15]. *Lord, who shall sojourn in thy tabernacle, and who shall dwell in thy holy mountain?* (i) *He who walks uprightly and* (ii) *works righteousness and* (iii) *speaks truth in his heart and* (iv) *has no slander on his tongue and* (v) *does no*

evil to his fellow and (vi) *does not take up a reproach against his neighbor,* (vii) *in whose eyes a vile person is despised but* (viii) *honors those who fear the Lord.* (ix) *He swears to his own hurt and changes not.* (x) *He does not lend on interest.* (xi) *He does not take a bridge against the innocent.* . . . .

Isaiah came and reduced them to six [Isaiah 33:25-26]: (i) *He who walks righteously and* (ii) *speaks uprightly,* (iii) *he who despises the gain of oppressions,* (iv) *shakes his hand from holding bribes,* (v) *stops his ear from hearing of blood* (vi) *and shuts his eyes from looking upon evil, he shall dwell on high.*

Micah came and reduced them to three [Micah 6:8]: *It has been told you, man, what is good, and what the Lord demands from you,* (i) *only to do justly and* (ii) *to love mercy, and* (iii) *to walk humbly before God.*

Isaiah again came and reduced them to two [Isaiah 56:1]: *Thus says the Lord,* (i) *Keep justice and* (ii) *do righteousness.*

Amos came and reduced them to a single one, as it is said, *For thus says the Lord to the house of Israel. Seek Me and live.*

Habakkuk further came and based them on one, as it is said [Habakkuk 2:4], *But the righteous shall live by his faith.*

Babylonian Talmud, Makkot, 24a

This long passage illustrates in both form and substance the very essential attributes of definitions of the halakhah seen all together. An emphasis is on the Hebrew Bible as the source of authoritative teaching. But the Scriptures are not cited in a slavish, unimaginative way. Rather, they are creatively used to serve as the raw material for the rabbi's own insights.

Now contrast these statements which Judaists would surely agree with—with the results of surveys of opinion cited in chapter 2:

[1] The Torah is the actual word of God: 13% concur [but so do 10% of born Jews with no religion; not a very impressive differential].

[2] The Torah is the inspired word of God, but not everything should be taken literally word for word; 38% of Judaists and 19% of the secularists concur.

[3] The Torah is an ancient book of history and moral precepts recorded by man; 45% of the Judaists and 63% of the secularist Jews concur.

By these figures, approximately half of all Judaists find no "ought" in the Torah, for out of history books flow no moral imperatives. Not only so, but how, out of what need not be taken literally, will Hillel's famous saying be translated into the here and now of obligation? Approximately four out of five Judaists (thus leaving only the Orthodox corner of the Judaic community over all, plus a handful of others) will recognize no norms to say what they have to do. What is not taken literally, word for word, is unlikely to yield well-worded rules of do's and don'ts: halakhah, the norm, the obligatory.

Let us take two specific cases in which by the two Judaisms that the people find self-evidently valid, we explain "why not that." The first is the simplest and may be treated cursorily: taking up Israeli citizenship and residence in the state of Israel. Migration from the United States and Canada for the first forty years of the life of the Jewish state has been miniscule. The Judaism of Holocaust and Redemption, in its North American formulation (there is a quite different Israeli version, which does not concern us) speaks of a pilgrimage to Auschwitz en route to Jerusalem. But it contains within itself no imperative to realize "redemption," meaning, to emigrate to the state of Israel and settle there.

A good Judaist will support Israel, maybe even send children to visit or even study for a semester. But the first and essential religious duty of Zionism, and also the principal religious obligation of the Israeli version of the Judaism of Holocaust and Redemption—to live in the state of Israel—that plays no role at all. To appeal to the Redemption part of the Judaism of Holocaust and Redemption, it suffices to formulate positive feelings about the state of Israel, even to participate in political action in its behalf. These are votive offerings—and votive offerings by definition are private, not obligatory.

A second obligation is prayer—not a few times on special occasions, but daily. The Judaists of North America believe in prayer, otherwise they would not participate in a Passover seder, marriage huppah, or the ineffable power of the liturgy of the Days of Awe. But they do not pray daily or even weekly, and here we have to explain another, fundamental "why not." Prayer is a much more complex example of the list of "why nots," and deserves close attention. In chapter 3, I offered in evidence of the self-evident plausibility of the Days of Awe the powerful liturgy that is recited in synagogue on those days. Matching the message with the moment, I claimed, explains why people come in droves to public worship on those days. But if we consider the liturgy of daily worship, we shall find the liturgy no less plausible. Indeed, if

I had to choose a single statement that I should predict would accord with the highest aspirations of Judaists, it would be daily prayer.

But prayer contains two components that render it "not necessary" for "a good Jew" to recite every day (three times a day no less). First, to pray every day, whether or not one feels like it (and that is the definition of daily prayer), imposes discipline in place of choice. And second, daily prayer, while relevant to the individual, encompasses also and especially the community.

That is why, in my view, Judaists list daily prayer among things only fanatics, the Orthodox, or remarkably holy people do. The conception that liturgy forms a labor in service of God that *we must do* whether we wish to do it or do not will not strike as alien at least some Christian communions. When Roman Catholic and Orthodox churches undertake the liturgy of reciting prayers in the conviction that the saying of those words bears sacred value and not only personal meaning, the same fundamental conception of public prayer as communal obligation pertains. And the centrality of prayer in most Protestant communions will make familiar the distinction between the votive and the obligatory in liturgy.

Still, that conception of public worship as obligatory, owing quite independent of the feelings and attitudes of the private individual, contradicts a commonly held view, characteristic of one wing of Protestant communions but not of the apostolic, historical and Reformation Protestant churches, on the one side, or of the Roman Catholic or Orthodox churches, on the other. It is that prayer is personal, expresses deepest emotions validated (or invalidated) within the individual heart, and is not primarily public, though people may do it together. God calls to each, and the individual responds to the call. Prayer takes place not as public performance of duty—recitation in common of the required words, sacrifice for the community at large, the carrying out of objective obligations—but responds to the heart and is the outpouring of the heart. Therefore prayer starts in private, and only then is shared. That is the opposite of an obligation incumbent on the community. For in that conception of prayer, the community hardly forms a significant component of the transaction—except after the fact.

Within this viewpoint prayer is something that individuals do by themselves and it is not duty but grace, not obligatory but optional in the deepest sense. Specifically, prayer, when possible, constitutes the human response to grace. From that point of view, saying the words mechanically whether of the *Hail Mary* or of the *Lord's Prayer* or of the *Shema,* makes no difference in heaven or on earth. But the priests of the ancient Temple and their continuators, the rabbis of the Mishnah and the Talmud and down to our own time, see prayer as public and communal. Everyone is engaged, says the words, sings the songs— however people feel that morning or that minute. The premise is that corporate society bears obligations to heaven, a part of which society as a whole carries out by saying the right words and making the right gestures.

People with no knowledge of a religious life lived out in corporate society, who see religion as, if not utterly personal, then fundamentally familial, can hardly expect themselves to recognize obligations to offer up, as a group, the recitation of certain words. The issue is not that offering up unfelt words taxes the imagination, while offering up compelling words makes sense. The same social experience that tells us why the vast majority of Jews form families to observe the Passover banquet rite explains why they do not ordinarily participate in public worship in the synagogue. Their social experience informs them that under the aspect of eternity, to be a Jew is to be part of a family, but tells them little in the aspect of their inner life about corporate responsibilities as a community.[3]

Some words evoke worlds, others do not, because some words refer to worlds we know, others speak of things we cannot recognize or identify. The individual in family understands life as metaphor. The family as part of community within the realm of religion does not. Corporate Israel exists in other dimensions, but not in the religious one. Consequently, the synagogue, which has served the very specific purpose of divine service to God through both the provision of public worship as is required of the community and the study of the Torah in public as is also demanded of the community, both changes and decays. It changes into a community center, flourishing (where it does) in those aspects of its program to which the holy words scarcely reach. It decays in that the service of the heart becomes lip service, words passively mumbled in suppression of utter incredulity. And that brings us to the words themselves.

The recitation of public prayers, obligatory for the community (as well as for the individual) encompasses three important matters: recitation of the creed, petition for the needs and welfare of the community and the individual, and the situation or identification of the community in its larger setting. I cannot imagine a more systematic or orderly exposition of that enchanted world precipitated by the recitation of the right words in the right way at the right time. The *Shema*—"Hear, O Israel, the Lord our God, the Lord is one"—presents the creed, hence the view of the world in its entirety. The *Shemoneh esré*—Prayer, or Eighteen Benedictions—covers the everyday needs of the community viewed in its own terms. The concluding prayer, *Alenu,* "It is our duty . . . ," then states the theory of Israel to which the worldview of the Shema and the way of life outlined in the Eighteen Benedictions refer.

Let us dwell on the recitation of the Shema and the Prayer, or Eighteen Benedictions. Only a direct encounter can convey the reason that in the holy books the liturgy forms the central task of all faithful Judaists, and, for the small Orthodox minority, forms the centerpiece of the religious life, along with the study of the Torah. Evening and morning, Israel individually and communally proclaims the unity and uniqueness of God. The proclamation is preceded and followed by blessings. The whole constitutes the credo of the Judaic tradition. It is "what the Jews believe." Components recur everywhere. The three elements of the creed cover creation, revelation, and redemption—that is to say, God as creator of the world, God as revealer of the Torah, and God as redeemer of Israel. The recital of the Shema is introduced by a celebration of God as creator of the world. In the morning, the individual, in community or not, recites these preliminary benedictions:

THE BLESSINGS RECITED BEFORE THE SHEMA

1. Creation of the World, attested by sunrise, sunset

Praised are You, O Lord our God, King of the universe.
You fix the cycles of light and darkness;
You ordain the order of all creation;
You cause light to shine over the earth;
Your radiant mercy is upon its inhabitants.

In Your goodness the work of creation
Is continually renewed day by day....
O cause a new light to shine on Zion;
May we all soon be worthy to behold its radiance.
Praised are You, O Lord, Creator of the heavenly bodies.[4]

The corresponding prayer in the evening refers to the setting of the sun:

Praised are You....
Your command brings on the dusk of evening.
Your wisdom opens the gates of heaven to a new day.
With understanding You order the cycles of time;
Your will determines the succession of seasons;
You order the stars in their heavenly courses.
You create day, and You create night,
Rolling away light before darkness....
Praised are You, O Lord, for the evening dusk.

Morning and evening, Israel responds to the natural order of the world with thanks and praise of God who created the world and who actively guides the daily events of nature. Whatever happens in nature gives testimony to the sovereignty of the Creator. And that testimony is not in unnatural disasters, but in the most ordinary events: sunrise and sunset. These evoke the religious response to set the stage for what follows.

For Israel, God is not merely Creator, but purposeful Creator. The works of creation serve to justify and to testify to Torah, the revelation of Sinai. Torah is the mark not merely of divine sovereignty, but of divine grace and love, the source of life here and now and in eternity. So goes the second blessing:

2. Revelation of the Torah as the expression of God's love for Israel

Deep is Your love for us, O Lord our God;
Bounteous is Your compassion and tenderness.
You taught our fathers the laws of life,
And they trusted in You, Father and king,
For their sake be gracious to us, and teach us,
That we may learn Your laws and trust in You.
Father, merciful Father, have compassion upon us:
Endow us with discernment and understanding.
Grant us the will to study Your Torah,
To heed its words and to teach its precepts....
Enlighten our eyes in Your Torah,
Open our hearts to Your commandments....
Unite our thoughts with singleness of purpose

To hold You in reverence and in love. . . .
You have drawn us close to You;
We praise You and thank You in truth.
With love do we thankfully proclaim Your unity.
And praise You who chose Your people Israel in love.

Here is the way in which revelation takes concrete and specific form in the Judaic tradition: God, the Creator, revealed his will for creation through the Torah, given to Israel his people. That Torah contains the "laws of life."

Moved to worship by the daily miracle of sunrise and sunset, corporate Israel responds with the prayer that Israel, like nature, may enjoy divine compassion. But what does that compassion consist of? The ability to understand and the will to study Torah. This is the mark of the relationship between God and the Jewish person: that his eyes are open to Torah and that his heart is open to the commandments. These are the means of divine service and of reverence and love for God. Israel sees itself as "chosen"—close to God—because of Torah, and it finds in its devotion to Torah the marks of its chosenness. The covenant made at Sinai—a contract on Israel's side to do and hear the Torah; on God's side, to be the God of Israel—is evoked by natural events and then confirmed by the deeds and devotion of corporate Israel. The corporate framework of the public prayers is implicit everywhere and explicit in the recurrent "we." We look in vain for the private person. What we see instead is the community affirming its obligation, carrying out its duty. In this context, those rites of passage upon which people focus with such intent appear somewhat trivial and personal, forming a stunning contrast to the majestic and public concern for the entirety of the cosmos and all of life.

THE RECITATION OF THE SHEMA

In the Shema, Torah leads Israel to enunciate the chief teaching of revelation:

Hear, O Israel, the Lord our God, the Lord is one.

This proclamation of the Shema is followed by three scriptural passages. The first is Deuteronomy 6:5-9:

*You shall love the Lord your God with all your heart, with all your soul, with
all your might.*

And further, one must diligently teach one's children these words and
talk of them everywhere and always, and place them on one's forehead,
doorposts, and gates. The second Scripture is Deuteronomy 11:13-21,
which promises that if Jews keep the commandments, they will enjoy
worldly blessings; but that if they do not, they will be punished and
disappear from the good land God gives them. The third is Numbers
15:37-41, the commandment to wear fringes on the corners of one's
garments. The fringes are today attached to the prayer shawl worn at
morning services by Conservative and Reform Jews, and worn on a
separate undergarment for that purpose by Orthodox Jews, and they
remind the Jew of *all* the commandments of the Lord.

The proclamation is completed and yet remains open, for having
created humanity and revealed his will, God is not unaware of events
since Sinai. Humanity is frail, and in the contest between the word of
God and the will of humanity, Torah is not always the victor. We
inevitably fall short of what is asked of us, and Jews know that their
own history consists of divine punishment for human failure time and
again. The theme of redemption, therefore, is introduced. Redemption—
in addition to creation and revelation, the third element in the tripartite
worldview—resolves the tension between what we are told to do and
what we are actually able to accomplish. In the end it is the theme of
God, not as Creator or Revealer, but as Redeemer that concludes the
twice-daily drama:

THE BLESSING RECITED AFTER THE SHEMA

3. Redemption of Israel then and in the future

You are our King and our fathers' King,
Our redeemer and our fathers' redeemer.
You are our creator....
You have ever been our redeemer and deliverer.
There can be no God but You....
You, O Lord our God, rescued us from Egypt;
You redeemed us from the house of bondage....
You split apart the waters of the Red Sea,
The faithful You rescued, the wicked drowned....

Then Your beloved sang hymns of thanksgiving. . . .
They acclaimed the King, God on high,
Great and awesome source of all blessings,
The everliving God, exalted in His majesty.
He humbles the proud and raises the lowly;
He helps the needy and answers His people's call. . . .
Then Moses and all the children of Israel
Sang with great joy this song to the Lord:
Who is like You, O Lord, among the mighty?
Who is like You, so glorious in holiness?
So wondrous Your deeds, so worthy of praise!
The redeemed sang a new song to You;
They sang in chorus at the shore of the sea,
Acclaiming Your sovereignty with thanksgiving:
The Lord shall reign forever and ever.
Rock of Israel, arise to Israel's defense!
Fulfill Your promise to deliver Judah and Israel.
Our redeemer is the Holy One of Israel,
The Lord of hosts is His name.
Praised are You, O Lord, redeemer of Israel.

Redemption is both in the past and in the future. That God not only creates but also redeems is attested by the redemption from Egyptian bondage. The congregation repeats the exultant song of Moses and the people at the Red Sea, not as scholars making a learned allusion, but as participants in the salvation of old and of time to come. Then the people turn to the future and ask that Israel once more be redeemed. But redemption is not only past and future. When the needy are helped, when the proud are humbled and the lowly are raised—in such commonplace, daily events redemption is already present. Just as creation is not only in the beginning, but happens every day, morning and night, so redemption is not only at the Red Sea, but every day, in humble events. Just as revelation was not at Sinai alone, but takes place whenever people study Torah, whenever God opens their hearts to the commandments, so redemption and creation are daily events. We note once more that while the individual may recite these prayers, the affirmation concerns the entire social entity, holy Israel.

The great cosmic events of creation in the beginning, redemption at the Red Sea, and revelation at Sinai—these are everywhere, every day near at hand. Israel views secular reality under the aspect of eternal, ever-recurrent events. What happens to Israel and to the world, whether good or evil, falls into the pattern revealed of old and made manifest each day. Historical events produce a framework in which future events will find a place and by which they will be understood. Nothing that happens cannot be subsumed by the paradigm.

Creation, the Exodus from Egypt, and the revelation of Torah at Sinai are commemorated and celebrated, not merely to tell the story of what once was and is no more, but rather to re-create out of the raw materials of everyday life the "true being"—life as it was, always is, and will be forever. At prayer Israel repeatedly refers to the crucial elements of its corporate being, thus uncovering the sacred both in nature and in history. In the proclamation of the Shema the particular events of creation—sunset, sunrise—evoke in response the celebration of the power and the love of God, of his justice and mercy, and of revelation and redemption.

◇————————————————————————◇

The Prayer, or Eighteen Benedictions

The Prayer, or Eighteen Benedictions, which the people recite standing and in silence, comes immediately after the immense statement of the creed in the Shema. These eighteen benedictions are petitions that directly address God with requests. What the community asks for— always in the plural—concerns the public welfare and covers matters we should today assign to the category of public policy as much as personal need. Some of these petitions, in particular those at the beginning and the end, recur in Sabbath and festival prayers.

The prayer of petition is said silently. Each individual prays by and for himself or herself, but together with other silent, praying individuals. The Eighteen Benedictions are then repeated aloud by the prayer leader, for the prayer is both private and public, individual and collective. To contemplate the power of these prayers imagine a room full of people, all standing by themselves yet in close proximity, some swaying this way and that, all addressing themselves directly and intimately to God in a whisper or in a low tone. They do not move their feet, for they are now standing before the King of kings, and it is not mete to shift and shuffle. If spoken to, they will not answer. Their attention is fixed upon the words of supplication, praise, and gratitude. When they begin, they bend their knees—so too toward the end—and at the conclusion they step back and withdraw from the Presence. Following are the words they say. The introductory three paragraphs define the One to whom petition is addressed, (1) the God of the founders, who is (2) omnipotent and (3) holy. The text of the three opening benedictions is as follows:

THE FOUNDERS:

Praised are you, Lord our God and God of our fathers, God of Abraham, God of Isaac, and God of Jacob, great, mighty, revered God, exalted, who bestow loving-kindness and are master of all things, who remember the acts of loyalty of the founders and who in love will bring a redeemer to their descendants for his great name's sake. King, helper, savior and shield, praised are you, Lord, shield of Abraham.

GOD'S POWER:

You are powerful for ever, Lord, giving life to the dead. You are great in acts of salvation. You sustain the living in loyalty and bring the dead to life in great mercy, holding up the falling, healing the sick, freeing the prisoners, and keeping faith with those who sleep in the dirt. Who is like you, Almighty, and who is compared to you, King who kills and gives life and brings salvation to spring up? And you are reliable to give life to the dead. Praised are you, Lord, who give life to the dead.

GOD'S SANCTITY:

We shall sanctify your name in the world just as they sanctify it in the heights of heaven. . . . Holy, holy, holy is the Lord of hosts, the whole earth is full of his glory. . . .

On weekdays petitionary prayer follows, covering these matters (the topic is given in bold, then the text of the prayer follows in italics). The concluding phrase, *Praised are You,* then marks the conclusion of the blessing at hand.

THE MAIN POINTS OF THE EIGHTEEN BENEDICTIONS RECITED ON WEEKDAYS

Wisdom-Repentance
You graciously endow man with intelligence;

You teach him knowledge and understanding.
Grant us knowledge, discernment, and wisdom.
Praised are You, O Lord, for the gift of knowledge.

Our Father, bring us back to Your Torah
Our King, draw us near to Your service;
Lead us back to You truly repentant.
Praised are You, O Lord, who welcome repentance.

Forgiveness-Redemption
Our Father, forgive us, for we have sinned;
Our King, pardon us, for we have transgressed;
You forgive sin and pardon transgression.
Praised are You, gracious and forgiving Lord.

Behold our affliction and deliver us
Redeem us soon for the sake of Your name,
For You are the mighty Redeemer.
Praised are You, O Lord, Redeemer of Israel.

Heal Us, Bless Our Years
Heal us, O Lord, and we shall be healed;
Help us and save us, for You are our glory.
Grant perfect healing for all our afflictions,
O faithful and merciful God of healing.
Praised are You, O Lord, Healer of Your people.

O Lord our God! Make this a blessed year;
May its varied produce bring us happiness.
Bring blessing upon the whole earth.
Bless the year with Your abounding goodness.
Praised are You, O Lord, who bless our years.

Gather Our Exiles, Reign Over Us
Sound the great shofar to herald [our] freedom;
Raise high the banner to gather all exiles;
Gather the dispersed from the corners of the earth.
Praised are You, O Lord, who gather our exiles.

Restore a wise and benevolent government.
Restore our judges as in days of old;
Restore our counsellors as in former times;
Remove from us sorrow and anguish.
Reign over us alone with lovingkindness;
With justice and mercy sustain our cause.
Praised are You, O Lord, King who loves justice.

Humble the Arrogant, Sustain the Righteous

Frustrate the hopes of those who malign us;
Let all evil very soon disappear;
Let all Your enemies be speedily destroyed.
May You quickly uproot and crush the arrogant;
May You subdue and humble them in our time.
Praised are You, O Lord, who humble the arrogant.

Let Your tender mercies, O Lord God, be stirred

For the righteous, the pious, the leaders of Israel,
Toward devoted scholars and faithful proselytes.
Be merciful to us of the house of Israel;
Reward all who trust in You;
Cast our lot with those who are faithful to You.
May we never come to despair, for our trust is in You.
Praised are You, O Lord, who sustain the righteous.

Favor Your City and Your People

Have mercy, O Lord, and return to Jerusalem, Your city;
May Your Presence dwell there as You promised.
Rebuild it now, in our days and for all time;
Reestablish there the majesty of David, Your servant.
Praised are You, O Lord, who rebuild Jerusalem.

Bring to flower the shoot of Your servant David.

Hasten the advent of the Messianic redemption;
Each and every day we hope for Your deliverance.
Praised are You, O Lord, who assure our deliverance.

O Lord, our God, hear our cry!

Have compassion upon us and pity us;
Accept our prayer with loving favor.
You, O God, listen to entreaty and prayer.
O King, do not turn us away unanswered,
For You mercifully heed Your people's supplication.
Praised are You, O Lord, who are attentive to prayer.

O Lord, Our God, favor Your people Israel

Accept with love Israel's offering of prayer;
May our worship be ever acceptable to You.
May our eyes witness Your return in mercy to Zion.
Praised are You, O Lord, whose Presence returns to Zion.

Our Thankfulness

We thank You, O Lord our God and God of our fathers,
Defender of our lives, Shield of our safety;

Through all generations we thank You and praise You.
Our lives are in Your hands, our souls in Your charge.
We thank You for the miracles which daily attend us,
For Your wonders and favor morning, noon, and night.
You are beneficent with boundless mercy and love.
From of old we have always placed our hope in You.
For all these blessings, O our King,
We shall ever praise and exalt You.
Every living creature thanks You, and praises You in truth.
O God, You are our deliverance and our help. Selah!
Praised are You, O Lord, for Your goodness and Your glory.

Peace and Well-Being
Grant peace and well-being to the whole house of Israel;
Give us of Your grace, Your love, and Your mercy.
Bless us all, O our Father, with the light of Your Presence.
It is Your light that revealed to us Your life-giving Torah,
And taught us love and tenderness, justice, mercy, and peace.
May it please You to bless Your people in every season,
To bless them at all times with Your fight of peace.
Praised are You, O Lord, who bless Israel with peace.

Now to see the Prayer as a whole: the first two petitions pertain to intelligence. Israel thanks God for knowledge of Torah, wisdom, and discernment. Discernment leads to the service of God and produces a spirit of repentance. We cannot pray without setting ourselves right with God, and that means repenting for what has separated us from God. Torah is the way to repentance and to return. So knowledge leads to Torah, Torah to repentance, and repentance to God. The logical next step is the prayer for forgiveness which is the sign of return. God is gracious and forgives sin. Once we discern what we have done wrong through the guidance of Torah, we seek to be forgiven. Sin leads to affliction. Affliction stands at the beginning of the way to God; once we have taken that way, we ask for our suffering to end; we beg redemption. We ask for healing, salvation, and a blessed year. Healing without prosperity means we may suffer in good health or starve in a robust body. So along with the prayer for healing goes the supplication for worldly comfort.

The individual's task is done. But what of the community? Health and comfort are not enough. The world is unredeemed. Jews are enslaved, in exile, and alien. At the end of days a great *shofar,* or ram's horn, will sound to herald the Messiah's coming. This is now besought. Israel at prayer asks first for the proclamation of freedom, then for the ingathering of the exiles to the Promised Land. Establishing the messianic kingdom, God needs also to restore a wise and benevolent government, good judges, good counsellors, and loving justice. Meanwhile Israel finds itself maligned. As the prayer sees things, arrogant men who hate Israel hate God as well. They should be humbled. And the pious and righteous—the scholars, the faithful proselytes, the whole house of Israel that trusts in God—should be rewarded and sustained. Above all, Israel remembers Jerusalem. They pray that the city would be rebuilt and they would dwell there, that God would set up Jerusalem's messianic king, David, and make him to prosper. These are the themes of the daily prayer: personal atonement, good health, and good fortunes; collective redemption, freedom, the end of alienation, good government, and true justice; the final and complete salvation of the land and of Jerusalem by the Messiah. Then they pray that their prayer may be heard and found acceptable; then an expression of thanksgiving, not for what may come, but for the miracles and mercies already enjoyed morning, noon, and night. At the end is the prayer for peace—a peace that consists of wholeness for the sacred community.

◇———————————————————————◇

Alenu: The Community Takes Leave

The third of the three components of the communal worship draws the community outward into the world. When Jews complete their service of worship, they mark the conclusion by making a statement concerning themselves in the world—the corporate community looking outward. Every synagogue service concludes with a prayer prior to going forth, called *Alenu,* from its first word in Hebrew: "It is incumbent upon us. . . ." Like the Exodus, the moment of the congregation's departure becomes a celebration of Israel's God, a self-conscious, articulated rehearsal of Israel's peoplehood. But now it is the end, rather than the beginning, of time that is important. When Jews go forth, they look forward:

It is incumbent on us to praise Him, Lord over all the world;
Let us acclaim Him, Author of all creation.
He made our lot unlike that of other peoples;
He assigned to us a unique destiny.
We bend the knee, worship, and acknowledge
The King of kings, the Holy One, praised is He.
He unrolled the heavens and established the earth;
His throne of glory is in the heavens above;
His majestic Presence is in the loftiest heights.
He and no other is God and faithful King,
Even as we are told in His Torah:
Remember now and always, that the Lord is God;
Remember, no other is Lord of heaven and earth.
We, therefore, hope in You, O Lord our God,
That we shall soon see the triumph of Your might,
That idolatry shall be removed from the earth,
And false gods shall be utterly destroyed.
Then will the world be a true kingdom of God,
When all mankind will invoke Your name,
And all the earth's wicked will return to You.
Then all the inhabitants of the world will surely know
That to You every knee must bend,
Every tongue must pledge loyalty.
Before You, O Lord, let them bow in worship,
Let them give honor to Your glory.
May they all accept the rule of Your kingdom.
May You reign over them soon through all time.
Sovereignty is Yours in glory, now and forever.
So it is written in Your Torah:
The Lord shall reign forever and ever.

We have spoken much of difference and how Jews have to cope with that fundamental fact of their lives. Having defined their corporate life in relationship to God in the Shema, to the community itself in the Prayer and in the Alenu, the community faces outward toward the nations.

Difference—in secular terms peoples' forming a separate, distinct group—here becomes destiny. Israel thanks God that it enjoys a unique destiny. But the community asks that he who made their lot unlike that of all others will soon rule as sovereign over *all*. The secular difference, which stands for the unique destiny, is only for the time being. When the destiny is fulfilled, there will be no further difference. The natural eye beholds a social group with some particular cultural characteristics defining that group. The myth of peoplehood transforms *difference* into *destiny*.

Having followed the transcendent sentiments of public, daily worship, the reader will grasp the urgency of the question: Why not that? For if the Day of Atonement plumbs the depths of guilt, punishment, atonement, and reconciliation, then daily prayer, three times no less, reaches still higher into heaven, and deeper into the soul. But, alas, it is not by choice but out of obedience to the commandment of the Torah, and that explains why not.

The premise of obligatory public worship is simple. The existence of the natural group means little, except as testimony to the sovereignty of the God who shaped the group and rules its life. The unique, the particular, the private are no longer profane matters of culture, but become testimonies of divine sovereignty, pertinent to all people, all groups. The particularism of the group is for the moment alone; the will of God is for eternity. When that will is done, all people will recognize that the unique destiny of Israel was intended for everyone. The ordinary facts of sociology no longer predominate. Theology takes over, in the mythic form, the story of eternal truths. The myth of Israel God's holy people has changed the secular and commonplace into the paradigm of true being. Public worship requires recitation of words that form worlds, and the words we have reviewed form a complete and cogent statement. But synagogues constituted for public worship succeed only seldom in filling their seats, and, for the most part, daily worship is conducted by a few heroic people. Most participants are obliged to recite the memorial *Qaddish* for the deceased. Even daily worship, therefore, so functions as to form an aspect of the life of the family.

Why should this be so? Not because one set of words makes more or less sense than another. The words of the prayers hardly appeal to beliefs less reasonable or less grounded in the perceived facts of the real world than the words that transform the rites of passage into reenactments of mythic being. Quite to the contrary, the creed, the petition, the prayer of departure contain affirmations of Israel as a supernatural entity before God, making a remarkably encompassing statement of the fundamental facts of existence as the faith defines them. As I have already suggested, we cannot appeal solely to the credible contents of one rite to explain its power or to the fantastic allegations of another rite to account for its neglect. Words work when the imagination makes them work. In our minds we make and therefore remake our world. Those words that in their primary propositions do retain powerful appeal address a circumstance that makes them welcome. The words that leave us Jews in general untouched and make no difference in shaping our world do not.

Words enchant in one setting, bore in another, because of their circumstance in which they are recited and the context in life's experience in which they are heard, not because of their propositions. The premise of prayer in the synagogue is simple: Public prayer is something we do together because it is our task. It is our task because we constitute corporate Israel and say our prayers as a community or a social entity. Synagogue prayers then create that social entity, that Israel, just as other prayers at life's passages call into being the world of Eden or through recalling Egypt and the Exodus express a certain resentment. But if we undertake the obligations we accept on our own volition and at our own option, not out of obligation at all, then words of public worship will create no worlds.

If prayer is what changes the "me" into the "us," and prayer is something we accomplish together because we have to, whether or not we feel it, then prayer will or will not evoke a world I know, depending on my social experience. Specifically, if I know no community beyond myself and my family, then words that evoke a corporate community will refer to a world I cannot imagine. Words that speak to my home and family will address a world I know, and therefore can reimagine in response to the right words.

Today Jews understand religion—that is, the Judaism of the dual Torah, for the Judaism of Holocaust and Redemption is not seen by them as a (competing) Judaic system at all—as essentially private and personal, since this is a generation of home and family, to which supernatural collectivities such as holy Israel, a corporate community before God, have little appeal. Experiences in life that everyone has, such as hunger and satisfaction, having a baby, feeling different, or getting married, undergo transformation because, to begin with, they refer to facts of life that are very real to us. But to what shared experience does public worship appeal, beyond an obligation to say the prayers? The fact that synagogues are empty from day to day and Sabbath to Sabbath shows that there is none. God lives for Israel—but not there. The fault lies not with the synagogue, surely not with the rabbi, who gives his or her life for Judaism, but with this-worldly Israel's social premise. What turns individuals and families into something larger than themselves, changing the "is" into a "what if" of a shared, social metaphor? It is a provocative question, which precipitates a self-evidently valid answer.

PART IV

So What?

A General Theory of
Why This, Not That, So What?

With a Concluding
Theological Postscript

◇

So what? What we learn concerns what it means to be religious in
North America (and elsewhere in the democratic and Protestant West).
Here in Protestant North America people commonly see religion as
something personal and private. Prayer, for example, speaks for the
individual. No wonder, then, that those enchanted words and gestures
recognize life's transitions and turn them into rites of passage. It is part
of a larger prejudice that religion and rite speak to the heart of the
individual.

What can be changed by rite then is first of all personal and private,
not social, not an issue of culture, not affective in politics, not part of
the public interest. What people do when they respond to religion affects
an interior world—a world with little bearing on the realities of public
discourse. The transformations of religion do not involve the world, or
even the self as representative of other selves, but mainly the individual
as the most unique and unrepresentative. If God speaks to me in
particular, then the message, by definition, is mine—not someone else's.
Religion, the totality of these private messages (within the present theory)
therefore does not make itself available for communication in public
discourse, and that by definition too. Religion plays no public role. It

is a matter not of public activity but of what people believe or do in private—a matter mainly of the heart.

When religion addresses what actually happens to people living together, and when the message it conveys conforms to their sense of self-evidence, then religion governs. What the books say will accurately describe what the people do. When religion pertains, but its message jars, people may do what the books say, but they may not do it in the way the books direct. And when the social order and the religious system do not correspond, then people will conclude "good Jews do this, not that." So what we learn is that religion lives in the perceived, social experience that people have; its ideas prove not right or wrong, not even persuasive or implausible, but self-evidently true because they are descriptive, or obviously irrelevant because they are not descriptive, of life as lived out in the social world. Conscience is the creation of community; theological truth is subject to the disposition of common sense, that is to say, a sense of what is fitting and just made common by being shared.

This generalization, which should not strike readers as new but only freshly instantiated in these pages, carries forward in an odd way the conviction of the Torah that God speaks to all Israel; the covenant is made with the holy people. Nor will the prophets have found surprising a descriptive way of expressing their certainty that God judges the community, not only the individual, and the you is always plural. "Our sages of blessed memory," the great religious geniuses who produced out of the oral Torah of Sinai the Mishnah, Talmuds, and Midrash compilations, took as their task the realization of the kingdom of priests and the holy people in the here and now of kitchens and bedrooms and marketplaces, and that is what their halakhah was, and is, all about.

So people cannot appeal to experience of a life in Israel and as Israel, an entire social entity, so as to validate the issues resolved by the rites of the corporate community, for example, the Sabbath and the synagogue. If the questions of community are not asked, not felt, not understood, the answers in rite give information no one needs or can use. That is why rites work; the cognitive ordering of the categories of time, space, action and community in rite takes place when individual imagination participates and does not take place when the experience of the individual in family as part of a larger social entity can be invoked. The deep can call only to depths where we have swum or crawled—but not to depths of experience no one has plumbed. "As if" depends on "is."

To do their work, the rites of faith have to form an answer to a question people want to ask. And urgent questions derive from experience: why this, not that—in regard to today, here and now, me and us? Basically people respond to the answers to questions they find inescapable. And then, in general, the substance of the answer will not make much difference to them, so long as the question is addressed. No answer proves more credible or less credible than any other, once the question has been asked. So the question answered by the Passover banquet rite concerns resentment of the Gentile, of the status of the minority, of the sense of difference. The answer transforms difference into destiny—slaves redeemed from Egypt indeed!—but then promises that, at some point, there will be no more differences. In form, both question and answer are communal and public. But in context, they address the individual in family, at home, not corporate Israel.

By contrast as we have seen, the Sabbath and festivals present powerful answers to the question people do not want to ask. The reason is that, in the context of the life of stratified society, the question proves too personal, the answer too penetrating. Who wishes to be told that what we have does not measure what we are? Not those who have. And, in yet another contrast, the Days of Awe, ask a question about my life, my fate, what has been and what is coming, that people do find pressing. They form a spell of remission, actually speaking of sin and pronouncing atonement, praying for forgiveness no one seriously imagines will be denied. The mythic language of a God on high, busily writing up each individual among the billions down below, does not provoke amusement but invokes awe, fear, reflection. It is because when people want to ask and answer a question, a deeply mythic mode will serve as well, or as (in)credibly, as any other. And that is the case even, as here, when the question is personal and private, the answer proves public and communal. Once more, therefore, the question proves the key. If the Sabbath and festivals address an unwanted answer to an unasked question, we can hardly expect holy days of sin and atonement to gain much entry into Jewry. But the opposite is the case.

I have pointed to the message contained in the rites that speak to the subjectivity and individuality of circumstance, lay stress on the private person, recognize and accord priority to the autonomous and autocephalic individual. What people find personally relevant they accept; for them, the words evoke meaning and make worlds. The rites that speak to the community out there beyond family, to the corporate existence of people who see themselves as part of a social entity beyond, scarcely resonate. The context therefore accounts for the difference and even for variations. Jews live one by one, family by family. Words that speak to that individuality work wonders. Jews do not form a corporate community but only families. Words that address the commonality of Israel not as the congregation of individual Jews but as a community bound by law to do some things together fall unheard, mere magic, not wonder-working at all.

What we learn about the religious life of North America from the fact that Jews really do respond to the holy occasions that speak of the individual and the family, while they have difficulty dealing with the ones that address the collectivity of public experience, then pertains not to Jews alone but to life in the open society created by Protestant Christianity and shared by Protestants with all comers, on terms of rough equality. The enchantment wrought by life in the democratic West should not be missed: the "I" even before God always remains the "I," and the "we" is just many "I"s formed into families. Israel before God is made up of Israelites, individual and family. For the sum of the whole is merely the same as the parts. But it is magic that makes the whole greater than the sum of the parts. In Judaism today that magic does not work, and the whole is not more, but less, than the sum of the parts. When holy Israel assembles in North America, a different Judaism takes over.

When we ask why there is a bifurcation between the personal and the familial—subjected to the Judaism of the dual Torah, perceived as religion—and the public and civic—governed by the Judaism of Holocaust and Redemption, perceived as politics—we turn outward. For the explanation lies in the definition of permissible difference in North America and the place of religion in that difference. Specifically, in North American society, defined as it is by Protestant conceptions, it is permissible to be different in religion, and religion is a matter of what is personal and private.

Hence Judaism as a religion encompasses what is personal and familial. But that definition of religion proves insufficient to cover Judaic religious systems that flourish, as we have seen. The Jews as a political entity then put forth a separate system, one that concerns not religion, which is not supposed to intervene in political action, but public policy. Judaism in public policy produces political action in favor of the state of Israel, or Soviet Jewry, or other important matters of the corporate community. Judaism in private affects the individual and the family and is not supposed to play a role in politics at all. That pattern conforms to the Protestant model of religion, and the Jews have accomplished conformity to it by the formation of two Judaisms. A consideration of the Protestant pattern, which separates not the institutions of church from the activities of the state, but the entire public polity from the inner life, will show us how to make sense of the presence of the two Judaisms of North America.

But the public life of Jewry, reaching religious statement in Judaism, is not trivial, not private, not individual, not a matter only of the heart. Religion is public, political, social, economic. As Goldscheider observes (in chapter 6 above), what marks the Jews as distinctive—therefore pointing toward those experiences that they share among themselves but not with outsiders—is social and cultural and economic. The Jews form a group not merely because they agree on certain propositions on which outsiders do not concur, but because they exhibit certain public traits that differentiate them from others. Religion as a powerful force in shaping politics and culture, economic action and social organization finds its counterpart, within Jewry, as we shall see, in the power of the community of the Jews to generate a Judaism.

Why then the stress in these pages on the social foundations of religious meaning? Because nothing humanity has made constitutes a less personal, a less private, a less trivial fact of human life than religion. Religion however is understood in Protestant North America as something private and interior, individual and subjective: how I feel all by myself, not what I do with other people. Religion is something you believe, all by yourself, not something you do with other people. The prevailing attitude of mind identifies religion with belief, to the near-exclusion of behavior. Religion is understood as a personal state of mind or an individual's personal and private attitude. When we study religion, the present picture suggests, we ask not about society but about self, not about culture and community but about conscience and character. Religion speaks of individuals and not groups; it is a matter of faith and its substance. William Scott Green further comments in more general terms as follows:

> The basic attitude of mind characteristic of the study of religion holds that religion is certainly in your soul, likely in your heart, perhaps in your mind, but never in your body. That attitude encourages us to construe religion cerebrally and individually, to think in terms of beliefs and the believer, rather than in terms of behavior and community. The lens provided by this prejudice draws our attention to the intense and obsessive belief called "faith," so religion is understood as a state of mind, the object of intellectual or emotional commitment, the result of decisions to believe or to have faith. According to this model, people have religion but they do not do their religion. Thus we tend to devalue behavior and performance, to make it epiphenomenal and of course to emphasize thinking and reflecting, the practice of theology, as a primary activity of religious people. . . . The famous slogan that "ritual recapitulates myth" follows this model by assigning priority to the story and to peoples' believing the story, and makes behavior simply an imitation, an aping, a mere acting out.[1]

As we reflect on Green's observations, we of course recognize what is at stake. It is the definition of religion, or, rather, what matters in or about religion, emerging from Protestant theology and Protestant religious experience.[2]

For when we lay heavy emphasis on faith to the exclusion of works, on the individual rather than on society, conscience instead of culture, when we treat behavior and performance by groups as less important and thinking, reflecting, theology and belief as more important, we simply adopt as normative for academic scholarship convictions critical to the Protestant Reformation. Judaism and the historical, classical forms of Christianity—Roman Catholic and Orthodox—place emphasis at least equally on religion as a matter of works and not faith alone, behavior and community as well as belief and conscience. Religion is something that people do, and they do it together. Religion is not something people merely have, as individuals. Since the entire civilization of the West, from the fourth century onward, carried forward the convictions of Christianity, not about the individual alone but about politics and culture, we may hardly find surprising the Roman Catholic conviction that religion flourishes not alone in heart and mind, but in eternal social forms: the church (in former times, the state as well).

A community of interest and experience such as the Jews comprise will self-evidently appeal to shared values that give expression to common experience, explaining in a single way how diverse individuals and families find it possible to see things in so cogent a manner: this way, not that. The issue, therefore, is not whether a Judaism forms the center, but *which* Judaism. What is important in understanding where and how Judaism is a religion and where it is not is this: two Judaisms coexist, one in private, the other in public. The Judaism of the dual Torah forms the counterpart to religion in the Protestant model, affecting home and family and private life. The Judaism of Holocaust and Redemption presents the counterpart to religion in the civil framework, making an impact upon public life and policy within the distinctive Jewish community of North America. The relationships between the two Judaisms prove parlous and uneven, since the Judaism of home and family takes second place in public life of Jewry—and public life is where the action takes place in that community.

Not only so, but the Judaism of the dual Torah makes powerful demands on the devotee, for example requiring him or her to frame emotions within a received model of attitudes and appropriate feelings. The Judaism of Holocaust and Redemption, by contrast, provides ready access to emotional or political encounters, easily available to all—by definition. The immediately accessible experiences of politics predominate. The repertoire of human experience in the Judaism of the dual Torah, by contrast, presents as human options the opposite of the immediate. In that Judaism Jews receive and use the heritage of human experience captured, as in amber, in the words of the dual Torah. That is why, in public life, Jews focus such imaginative energies as they generate upon "the Holocaust," and they center their eschatological fantasies on "the beginning of our redemption" in the state of Israel. Two competing Judaisms, the one that works at home, the other in public, therefore coexist on an unequal basis, because the one appeals to easily imagined experience, the other to the power of will to translate and transform the here and the now into something other.

◇ ── ◇

A Concluding Theological Postscript

And yet—if I may shade over into theology and make my conviction and judgment explicit—the Judaism of the Holocaust and Redemption, with its focus upon the out-there of public policy and its present paramountcy, offers as a world nightmares made of words. Its choice of formative experiences, its repertoire of worthwhile human events— these impose upon Jews two devilish enchantments. First, the message of Holocaust and Redemption is that difference is not destiny but disaster—if one trusts the Gentiles.

Second, the media of Holocaust and Redemption, political action, letters to public figures, pilgrimages to grisly places—leave the inner life untouched but distorted. Being Jewish in that Judaism generates fear and distrust of the other, but it does not compensate by an appeal to worth and dignity for the self. The Judaism of Holocaust and Redemption leaves the life of individual and family untouched and unchanged. But people live at home and in family. Consequently, the Judaism of Holocaust and Redemption in ignoring the private life makes trivial the differences that separate Jew from Gentile. People may live a private life of utter neutrality, untouched by the demands of the faith, while working out a public life of acute segregation. The Judaism of Holocaust and Redemption turns on its head the wise policy of the reformers and enlightened of the early nineteenth century: a Jew at home, a citizen out there. Now it is an undifferentiated American at home, a Jew in the public polity.

The Judaism of the dual Torah, for its part, proves equally insufficient. Its address to the self and family to the near-exclusion of the world beyond leaves awry its fundamental mythic structure, which appeals to history and the end of time, to sanctification and the worth of difference. Viewed whole, each of its components at the passage of life and the passing of one's own life—the disposition of birth, marriage, aging—makes sense only in that larger context of public policy. Separating the private and familial from the public and communal distorts the Judaism of the dual Torah. Ignoring the individual and the deeply felt reality of the home leaves the Judaism of Holocaust and Redemption strangely vacant, in the end a babble of tear-producing but unfelt words, a manipulation of emotions.

What can draw people together and persuade them in public, not only in private, to do one thing and not another and move them and shape their hearts—and also their minds? When we locate the appropriate medium for enchantment, the message for that medium will dictate itself. That medium must now move beyond mere words, into the world of poetry, drama, and theater. The world of art and the arts awaits to do its wonder.

To state matters simply, in my view the future of a single Judaism, public and private, will begin when media beyond words alone so take shape as to impart to Jewry a Judaism of experience that encompasses both the message of the dual Torah and the anguished memory, so near at hand and painful, of our sorrow and our joy in Europe and in the state of Israel. Through art Jews will move from worlds made out of words to worlds transformed in imagination and the educated, inner eye.

I may say very simply what I think people should do, since the medium will shape the message. The synagogue—for in the end Jewry will live or die in the synagogue, which is where they are different from everyone else—must turn itself into a theater, but one of a very special order. The congregation must transform itself into a company of actors and also a choir. Choreography must dictate the grace of the community through processional and mime. The arts of the artists of the day must educate vision for the synagogue—no more sheets of artificial walnut or walls of untouched brick. We must learn to see the "as if" in the "is," as did the sages who read Scripture and heard a message about the politics of their age.

Since the arts transform life into metaphor and through the power of will and the force of imagination change "is" into "might be," the very public experience of "being Jewish" in sentiment and sensibility emerges from the mind moving upward when mere words fail: movement beyond message made up of mere words. The message emerges from the moment of pure and holy recognition: yes, that is what it is all about, that is what it means. In that shared perception prior to words and beyond them, creation begins for the world that awaits.

Do I see things that, in practical terms, should change? I do indeed. Today's Jewish community conducts business principally through propaganda, understood as the medium of the printed word in prose, as though little has changed in the art of communication since the invention of printing. Though the Jews helped create the art of the moving image—the cinema—Jews transmit their traditions without teaching their children to express "being Jewish" with the moving image, videocamera in hand for instance. Jews in advertising understand the power of the unarticulated symbol, but Jews in the synagogue persist in word-mumbling and word-mongering as the sole form of worship. Jews stand in the forefront of all of the international worlds of the arts in America and Europe, but Jewry as a matter of public policy has yet to recognize the profoundly artistic gifts within Jewry, on the one side, and the deep response, of Jewry, to the arts, on the other.

That explains why, for the most part, when we Jews wish to formulate and express a Jewish message, we resort to words—and then to words of a particular sort: printed, rather than spoken; prose, rather than poetry; fact, rather than fiction for example. James Michener in *The Source* taught more people Jewish history than Salo W. Baron in *A Social and Religious History of the Jews*, the one through sketches of light and shadow, narrative and craft, the other through endless paragraphs of heavy, unfelt words. The theology of Cynthia Ozick, like that of John Updike for Protestant Christianity, informs culture. We cannot say the same of the theology of a single living Judaic theologian, and of only a single theologian of Judaism in our century in North America, Abraham J. Heschel.

The Jewish school ordinarily teaches as though television did not exist and as though most people acquired most of what they know in the printed word. Yet we live in the age of television and video, we understand the arts of persuasion through image, we appreciate the power of poetry, we appeal to the force of design arts, we acquire knowledge from what we see and hear at least as much as from what we read, and, in all, we understand that life is a theater without walls and that drama takes place all around us. To judge by the growth of semiotics as a disciplined field of learning, the coming century will speak as much through symbol and image, gesture and mime, as our ancestors spoke through the Word translated mainly into words. But the Jewish community has yet to learn the first lesson of the age of the global village, which is that the medium is the message.

The arts, with their appeal to the heart and soul when words fail, form the medium for the coming messages of Judaism, the mode of enchantment beyond words. For the arts grasp how to speak through movement and gesture, song and poetry, voice and silence, music for the ear and heart, art for the eye and soul. The arts can take a stone and make a sculpture that will move us; they can take our stony hearts and open them to the depths. Judaism works because of its capacity to turn social fact into fantasy. *We are Jews because of the power of our imagination.*

To be a Jew is at its foundations an act of art. It is to perceive the ordinary as simile and the received as metaphor. It is to turn what we are through will and heart and soul into something more than we imagine we can be. Jews' task is to make ourselves into works of art. This act of surpassing art we do through poetry, drama, music, dance— the arts of the eye and the arts of the soul and the arts of the folk alike. Setting the Sabbath table is an act of art. Carrying the Torah in the synagogue processional is an act of dance. Composing a prayer and reciting a prayer are acts of poetry and drama. The memorial and commemoration of the murder of six million Jews in Europe take the form of film and fiction even now. All of these point the way in which we must go.

It is the arts' enchantment of Jewish existence, worked through poetry, not prose; music, not uncadenced speech; that transforms one thing into something else. For our human existence as Jews requires us to turn one place, in the here and now, into another place, in time to come or times past and always, a thing into a different thing— humanity into God's image and after God's likeness, the ultimate transformation of creation. Time becomes a different time, space a different place, gesture and mime more than what they seem, assembled people a social entity, a being that transcends the human beings gathered together—a nation, a people, a community. Scripture, prayers, formulas of faith—these form mere words. They define categories other than the ones contributed by the here and now.

For the world in all its prosaic and factual messages does not tell us who we are or what we are. It tells us the opposite. It does not affirm our worth. At best the world ignores, at worst the world denies, that worth. We are a small people, yet we imagine that we matter. We are a people of little account, yet we tell ourselves we come from Abraham,

Isaac, Jacob, Sarah, Rebecca, Leah, and Rachel. That is why we have
to resort to that inner world of imagination made real by art. For the
world is there for us to defy, our task is to undertake pretense like the
pretense of the theater.

That task of sculpting life into art and imagining life as it must be
begins not in politics but in theology, when, in Scripture, we read: "Let
us make man in our image, after our likeness." To see a human being
and to perceive God—that is what it means to be a Jew, so Scripture
says. And that is an act of art, a moment of artistic truth, to be carried
out alone by poetry, not by prose; alone by theater, not by ordinary
speech; alone by dance, not by clumsy and ordinary shuffling; alone by
the silence of disciplined sound we know as music, not by background
noise and rackets; alone by the eye of the artist who sees within and
beyond, not by the vacant stare of those who do not even see what is
there.

To be a Jew is to live both "as if" and also in the here and now.
By "as if" I mean that we form in our minds and imaginations a picture
of ourselves that the world we see every day does not sustain. We are
more than we seem, other than we appear to be. To be a Jew is to live
a metaphor, to explore the meaning of life as simile, of language as
poetry and action as drama and vision as art. For Scripture begins with
the judgment of humanity that we are "in our image, after our likeness,"
and once humanity forms image and likeness, then, to begin with, we
are not what we seem but something different, something more. And
for Israel, the Jewish people, the metaphor takes over in the comparison
and contrast between what we appear to be and what in the image,
after the likeness of the Torah, we are told we really are.

Words merely refer to revelation, appeal to God, not merely make
explicit but affirm attitude and feeling and trust. Standing for acceptance
and submission, response and renewal and regeneration, in the end
words in Judaism therefore are not the thing, the religion, but merely
the name of the thing, the notes, as I said, that tell us how to make
the religion. Judaism works its wonder upon time, space, deed, assembly,
through word and gesture, song and speech, denoting persons, things,
God—throughout, in art. Definite, objective rules, set sequences of
words and acts, work the wonder of enchantment, turning water into
wine, family assembled for a meal into slaves escaping from Egypt, and
common folk into Israel, God's people, each in its proper time and

place. And it is how, too, we endure the six million murders, one by one, that torment us every day. That too forms an act of imagination nourished by the right words, said in the right way.

That is not to say the words form mere mumbled incantation. Far from it. The words convey propositions, and rites stand for truths that we can express. But Judaic existence is not in the words, the emotions, and the attitudes alone. Judaism takes place through the arts, in enchantment that transforms, changing something into something else, somewhere into anywhere, some time into all time. And therefore we cannot say that Judaism *is*, rather, Judaism *takes place* at that moment at which in our imagination, expressed through media of heart and intellect beyond all speech, we enter into the circle of the sacred and through words of enchantment transform the world, if only for a moment. That is where God takes place.

> *To form—to be—Israel is an act of imagination and will.*
> *For a Jew, it is a sin to despair.*

Notes to Preface

1. To show how the religions of the world have rooted themselves in this country, I have edited the textbook *World Religions in Today's America* (Louisville: Westminster/John Knox Press, forthcoming).

2. New York: Basic Books, 1987. Second printing. Atlanta: Scholars Press, 1991.

3. A stunning instance is Steven M. Cohen, *Content or Continuity? Alternative Bases for Commitment* (New York: The American Jewish Committee, 1991). As we shall see in chapter 2, Cohen went over exactly the same questions in 1991 that I treated in 1987—four years earlier—without responding to the analysis and thesis I had set forth. On the subject at hand, Cohen's is by far the best work in an intellectually shoddy and dismal field to be sure.

Notes to Chapter 2

1. This does not mean, I could not find data on how many Orthodox or Conservative or Reform Jews do such-and-such a rite. Studies of Orthodox and Conservative Jews do ask some of the questions that interest us, in particular, those of Orthodox Jews. But my interest is in the description of the behavior of all Judaists, not only some, and my problem is to explain how Jews who are also Judaists compose a Judaism. If, in its context, I wanted to know about

Orthodox Judaic behavior, some of the studies we have in hand amply and (I think) accurately describe that, with full surveys and statistics; Samuel Heilman's work, listed below, is exemplary. But then, if I wanted to explain Orthodox Judaic behavior, I should have to start with the holy books, which is where Orthodoxy starts; and I should have little basis for contrasting what the books say with what the people do.

2. I consulted a variety of books and articles, but mainly rely upon Steven M. Cohen, *Content or Continuity? Alternative Bases for Commitment* (New York: American Jewish Committee, 1991); Jack Wertheimer, "Recent Trends in American Judaism," *American Jewish Year Book, 1989* (hereafter, Wertheimer); and Barry A. Kosmin, Sidney Goldstein, Joseph Waksberg, Nava Lerer, Ariella Keysar, and Jeffrey Scheckner, *Highlights of the CJF [Council of Jewish Federations] 1990 National Jewish Population Survey* (New York: Council of Jewish Federations, 1991) (hereafter, Kosmin). Michael Satlow provided, in addition, these items: M. Sklare and J. Greenblum, *Jewish Identity on the Suburban Frontier: A Study of Group Survival in the Open Society* (New York: Basic Books, 1967), pp. 49-96; Charles Liebman and S. Shapiro, "A Survey of the Conservative Movement and Some of Its Religious Attitudes" (unpublished manuscript, New York, 1979), pp. 17-24; Samuel Heilman and Steven M. Cohen, *Cosmopolitans and Parochials: Modern Orthodox Jews in America* (New York: Basic Books, 1987), pp. 39-111, 207-16, 222-27, 235-44; Samuel Heilman and Steven M. Cohen, "Ritual Variation among Modern Orthodox Jews in the United States," *Studies in Contemporary Jewry* 2:164-87; and Steven M. Cohen, *American Assimilation or Jewish Revival?* (Bloomington: Indiana University Press, 1988), pp. 71-81, 130. Professor Calvin Goldscheider provided the following: Calvin Goldscheider, "Jewish Individuals and Jewish Communities: Using Survey Data to Measure the Quality of American Jewish Life" (unpublished manuscript, prepared for the Third Sydney Hollander Memorial Conference on Policy Implications of the 1990 National Jewish Population Survey, July 1991); Calvin Goldscheider, "The Structural Context of American Jewish Continuity: Social Class, Ethnicity, and Religion" (unpublished paper presented at the American Sociological Association, Cincinnati, 1991); Steven M. Cohen, *Content or Continuity? Alternative Bases for Commitment. The 1989 National Survey of American Jews* (New York: American Jewish Committee, 1991). Note also Gary A. Tobin, "From Alarms to Open Arms," *Hadassah Magazine,* December, 1991, pp. 22ff.; Arthur J. Magida, "The Pull of Passover," *Baltimore Jewish Times,* April 17, 1992, pp. 58ff.; Samuel C. Heilman, *Jewish Unity and Diversity: A Survey of American Rabbis and Rabbinical Students* (New York: American Jewish Committee, 1991).

3. "A Survey of the Conservative Movement and Some of Its Religious Attitudes" (see n. 2, above).

4. Cohen, *American Assimilation or Jewish Revival?* p. 80.

5. Cohen, *American Assimilation or Jewish Revival?* p. 81.

6. Cohen, *Content or Continuity? Alternative Bases for Commitment* (see n. 2, above), p. 4. Cohen distinguishes between "the Jewish-identity patterns of the more involved and passionate elites [and] those of the more numerous, marginally affiliated Jews, those with roughly average levels of Jewish involvement and emotional investment.... One may be called 'commitment to content' and the other 'commitment to continuity.' Alternatively ... 'commitment to ideology' versus 'commitment to identity.' "

7. Ibid., pp. 14–15.

8. Ibid., p. 21.

9. Ibid., pp. 41-42.

Note to Chapter 3

1. Translations in this chapter follow Jules Harlow, ed., *Daily Prayerbook* (New York: Rabbinical Assembly, 1978).

Note to Chapter 4

1. The translations from the Passover Narrative (Haggadah) are my own, but I follow the text of Maurice Samuel, *The Passover Haggadah* (New York: 1942), and I consulted his translations throughout.

Notes to Chapter 5

1. The same disparity between the books and the peoples' broadly held sense of how things are supposed to be accounts for the creation, in North American Judaism, of the dietary customs called all together "kosher-style." "Kosher-style" means no pork or shrimp, but also no requirement for meat from properly slaughtered beasts, no separate dishes for dairy and meat, and few of the other rules of kosher preparation of suitable food. The anomaly came to the fore at Brandeis University, when, responding to the desires of non-Jewish students, at the trustees' instance, the president agreed that the University's non-kosher dining rooms (it had kosher ones in any event) might serve shrimp and pork, Asian and black students having asked for "their" food too. A huge uproar at this "dejudaization" of Brandeis followed, with the argument that these are foods Jews do not eat, therefore they should not be served. The reply that the Torah does not require Gentiles to observe the dietary laws—and an unkosher dining room is just that—elicited an utterly unbelieving response. The given

of the people concerning dietary laws demanded more—and of the wrong people—than the rules of the books. The people's practiced Judaism prevailed, and shrimp and pork were banned, although the unkosher dining rooms remained unkosher of course, still serving cheeseburgers, which by definition are unkosher, with their mixture of dairy and meat products, but not lobster. The fiasco fizzled out with the trustees' blaming the president, whom they fired.

2. If it is a fact, I could find no current statistics on the practice and rely on (naturally, unsubstantiated) impressions and hearsay.

3. Admittedly, a considerable qualification; but I do maintain ideas count, attitudes matter, and what the liturgy says, people do hear. The intense religious environment of the New Year and Day of Atonement, on the one side, and Passover, on the other, make no sense at all if people are just going through motions. And the one thing the rabbis do well is repeat what "the tradition" says. (True, it may be "the tradition" as they make it up that morning, but the holy books do gain a hearing, if not always a full, informed and accurate one.)

4. As I said, I could not find current figures on how broadly the rite is practiced among Judaists. Hearsay suggests Reform Jews conduct the rite through surgeons in hospitals, Conservatives sometimes there, sometimes in a religious setting at home, and Orthodox always as the books say. Nor could I find current figures to tell us how large a proportion of male Jewish babies are circumcised at all. Hearsay continues to suggest that nearly all are.

5. Lifsa Schachter, "Reflections on the Brit Mila Ceremony," *Conservative Judaism* 1986, 38:38–41.

6. *Pirke deRabbi Eliezer*, trans. Gerald Friedlander (London, 1916), pp. 212–214.

7. Schachter, "Reflections," p. 41.

8. Here again, I could find no current statistics and speak only from impressions. Since Judaists ordinarily belong to synagogues, for a Judaist not to celebrate a bar or bat mitzvah would present a surprise; not only so, but the pattern of synagogue membership is for families to belong when children are growing up, then to drop membership after the bar or bat mitzvah. That pattern again points toward wide popularity for this rite. It also underscores my insistence that the peoples' practice knows nothing of covenant and obligation, two points on which the books insist.

9. I found nothing in the current reports that indicates how many marriages between two Jews professing Judaism are performed by a rabbi or a cantor, and how many by a justice of the peace or a judge; my impression is that,

under such circumstances, secular marriage is very uncommon. To the contrary, rabbis are commonly asked to "officiate" when a Jew marries a Gentile, and a majority of all Reform rabbis do so. So it appears that the people want what the books do not provide—a Judaic rite when a Jew marries out.

10.   Here too, I could find no evidence to substantiate that impression. Nor do I know how many Jews bury their dead in other-than-Jewish cemeteries. I rely on general impression that when Jews die, they are buried with rabbis in attendance, and in Jewish burial grounds. I also do not know the proportion of Jews who accept cremation, which is prohibited by book Judaism (it stands for the denial of the physical resurrection of the dead, which the classical Judaic doctrine affirms). My impression is that a higher proportion of Jews want Judaic rites for funerals than object to cremation (or the "harvesting" of body parts for reuse). A mark of the disinterest of social science in Judaism, the religion, is the rather substantial set of questions on religious practice among Jews that we cannot answer out of the results of social science.

11.   Such a couple would testify to militant secularism, a position that has become rare within the Jewish community. Two generations ago, it was a common position, taken over, so it seems to me, by the formation of a "secular" or "humanistic" Judaism, on the one side, and by elements of Reform and Conservative Judaism, on the other.

12.   No sociologist—predictably—has asked whom people invite to this or to that, even when asking about friendship- and associational-patterns.

13.   Jules Harlow, ed., *A Rabbi's Manual* (New York: Rabbinical Assembly, 1965), p. 32.

14.   Ibid., p. 130.

15.   These customs may or may not be broadly followed. It is clear that book Judaism does not always describe practiced Judaism in funerary rites. For example, Judaism has no provision for an open coffin, which morticians recommend and an indeterminate number of Jews prefer. Burial in the state of Israel, which is done under Orthodox auspices, involves only shrouds—no coffins; pouring dirt on the wrapped-up body of a loved one is a jarring experience, to say the least.

16.   The literature that I surveyed, with the help of consultations with others, covers the past decade and the main community-wide surveys, as cited in chapter 2. I know for certain that no such survey included questions on funerary practice. Beyond that, I claim only impressions of the state of research. I should gladly stand correction. An examination of my principal sources—Jack Wertheimer, "Recent Trends in American Judaism," *American Jewish Year Book, 1989*; and Barry A. Kosmin, Sidney Goldstein, Joseph Waksberg, Nava Lerer,

Ariella Keysar, and Jeffrey Scheckner, *Highlights of the CJF [Council of Jewish Federations] 1990 National Jewish Population Survey*—will show the character of information we now have in hand, which, for the study of Judaism as practiced, is exceedingly sparse.

Notes to Chapter 6

1. The problem then is to explain the principle of choice, and my solution emerges as we proceed. Let me briefly signal the entire exposition. This is in two aspects. First, "why this, not that" in the menu of book Judaism? Second, "why this, not that" in the menu of the Judaism of Holocaust and Redemption? And the answers are in two parts also. In book Judaism, as I have now fully set forth, "this" will concern private life, "that" will concern corporate life; and, among the things people do, the congruence of the message of the rite to the social experience or desired social experience of the Judaist governs. That explains kosher as against kosher-style, a rite of circumcision as against a surgical operation. In the Judaism of Holocaust and Redemption, "this" that people do is selected against "that" that people do not do for equally self-evident considerations, as I shall suggest both in this chapter and in the next.

2. Calvin Goldscheider, *Jewish Continuity and Change: Emerging Patterns in America* (Bloomington: Indiana University Press, 1986), p. 170.

3. Ibid., p. 171.

4. I have to avoid the word "myth" because of its use by today's anti-Semites to deny that Jews were murdered by the Germans, or murdered in the numbers people say, or were murdered in death factories (starvation and abuse seem to them less evil). In this context, "the myth of Holocaust and Redemption," which is language suitable in the study of religion, proves inappropriate.

5. That is not to suggest American Judaism constitutes a version of Zionism. Zionism maintains that Jews who do not live in the Jewish state are in exile. There is no escaping that simple allegation, which must call into question that facile affirmation of Zionism central to American Judaism. Zionism further declares that Jews who do not live in the state of Israel must aspire to migrate to that nation or, at the very least, raise their children as potential emigrants. On that position American Judaism chokes. Zionism moreover holds that all Jews must concede, indeed affirm, the centrality of Jerusalem, and of the state of Israel, in the life of Jews throughout the world. Zionism draws the necessary consequence that Jews who live outside the state of Israel are in significant ways less "good Jews" than the ones who live there. Now all of these positions, commonplace in Israeli Zionism and certainly accepted, in benign verbal formulations to be sure, by American Jews, contradict the simple facts of the

situation of American Jews and their Judaism. First, they do not think that they are in exile. Their Judaism makes no concession on that point. Second, they do not have the remotest thought of emigrating from America to the state of Israel. That is so even though in ceremonial occasions they may not protest when Israelis declare that to be their duty.

6. We return to this matter in chapter 8.

Notes to Chapter 7

1. People may well find excessive that description of the rather humble and ordinary events I have treated, e.g., a family dinner, a surgical rite. But religion transforms what is common and makes it holy, at least, for Judaism. Whether I generalize out of a case or offer a truly viable generalization I do not claim to know. This is only one of the many points of ignorance that form the agenda of this chapter and the next, but, then, theory is that way.

2. Remember, I speak of "why this, not that," not "why this person, not that person." I do not address that distinct, but equally interesting question. So, I hasten to add, I do not pretend to know why people who have the same social experience, e.g., of the life cycle or of exclusion and anti-Semitism, do not invariably respond in the same way, that is, through rites of the life cycle or through the Passover seder. Why among those with the same social experience, e.g., of the same ethnic group, some people are religious and others not I really cannot say. Whether or not the answer will have to come from psychology, not sociology, or from theology, not history I cannot say; I can imagine for myself diverse explanations, from each of these disciplines, but I cannot choose among them. My guess is that, for the faithful, theology provides the best answers, and, for the other, psychology reduces the social question to very personal dimensions. For the purpose of this book I do not have to choose. For I claim to explain what is, not what isn't: why people who do one thing do not do some other, not why people do not do the things they do not do. In any case, we are never responsible to explain what other people think about themselves or the world.

3. That is not to suggest they do not form a corporate community. In politics, in history, in society, even in economics, they do. But the realm of the sacred touches their passage through life and draws them into contact with others principally through home and family.

4. For the Prayer, I follow the translation of Jules Harlow, *Daily Prayerbook*.

Notes to Chapter 8

1. William Scott Green, personal correspondence, January 17, 1985.

2. I hasten to add, I refer not to the Protestant Christianity that the books describe, but to the Protestant Christianity that Protestants put forth in the here and now of our society: a religion that not uncommonly begins in the radical conversion of the individual in a direct and fresh encounter with God. Being "saved by Jesus" in the part of America I inhabit and deeply value is an intensely personal encounter with God—an encounter as intense as mine with the Torah. The experience of conversion stands at the gate of a community, to be sure, but in the liturgical vocabulary of Protestant communions as an "I" that Judaism does not recognize. The saying, "you cannot make the Sabbath" by yourself has no counterpart in a religion that has God speak to humanity one by one. It would be an exaggeration to say that Protestants meet God retail, Judaists (and, I think, Catholics and Orthodox Christians) wholesale, but that is what things appear to be—not by the evidence of what the books say, but only what the people do.

GENERAL INDEX

◇―――――――――――――――――――◇

――――――――――――― ◇ ―――――――――――――

American-Israel Political Action
    Committee, 108
Anti-Semitism, 47, 67
    Holocaust and Judaism of
        redemption, 108-19

Bar and bat Mitzvah, 46, 59, 87-93
Baron, Salo W., *A Social and
    Religious History of the Jews*,
    162
Buddhism, 22-23
Bullock, Allan, *Parallel Lives*, 24-25

Charities, support of, 43-44
Circumcision, 7, 17, 36, 45-47, 59,
    78-86, 109, 123
Cohen, Steven M., 42-43, 45-47
Community life, 124-28, 134, 140-
    45, 154-65
Conservative Judaism, adult Jews'
    adherence to, 40-42
Contemporary religion, choice of
    beliefs, 13-29

Creation, 7
Crossan, John Dominic, *The
    Historical Jesus: The Life of a
    Mediterranean Jewish Peasant*,
    25

Day of Atonement (Yom Kippur),
    8-9, 41, 43-45, 47, 53-54, 56, 59
Days of Awe, 53-57, 59, 132, 155
Death: *See* Funerary rites
Dietary laws
    everyday variations, 14-15, 20-21
    kosher foods, 41-43, 45
    as sanctification, 20
Doctrines
    living religious life, 17
    theology and what people do,
        150-65

Eighteen Benedictions, 12, 135, 140-
    45
Ethnicity, social aspects of North
    American Jewish people, 30-48

175

Fackenheim, 114, 125
Family and observances, 63-76, 123-28
  circumcision, 7, 17, 36, 45-47, 59, 78-86, 109, 123
  funerary rites, 46, 59-60, 103-7
  matriarchal lineage, 33
  Passover seder, 7, 10, 41-44, 46-47, 51-52, 57-59, 61, 63-75, 123, 125, 155
Feast of Tabernacles (Sukkot), 8, 51, 57-59, 61
Funerary rites, 46, 59-60, 103-7
  confession at onset of death, 104-5
  kaddish, prayer for sanctification, 105-6
  "sitting shiva," 107

Goldman, Ari L., 41-44, 46-47
Goldschheider, Calvin, 112, 157
Greeley, Andrew, 125
Green, William Scott, 158

Hanukkah, 52, 63, 75-76, 125
Heschel, Abraham J., 162
Holocaust
  and Judaism of redemption, 108-19, 124-28, 148, 155-59
  symbol of Jewish life, 47
Home and family observances, 7, 11-12, 63-76, 123-28
  circumcision, 7, 17, 36, 45-47, 59, 78-86, 109, 123
  funerary rites, 46, 59-60, 103-7
  Passover seder, 7, 10, 41-44, 46-47, 51-52, 57, 59, 61, 63-75, 123-25, 155

Individuality, 7, 11

religious beliefs and social practices, 153-65
rites of passage affecting, 10

Jesus
  man of history and faith, 20-26
  The Historical Jesus: The Life of a Mediterranean Jewish Peasant (Crossan), 25
  A Marginal Jew: Rethinking the Historical Jesus (Meier), 24
Jewish people
  ethnicity and religiousness, 30-48
  matriarchal lineage, 33
  sociological examination of North American Jewish people, 30-48
Judaists, denominational preferences, 40-42, 44

Kaddish. funerary prayer for sanctification, 105-6
Kaplan, Mordecai M., 125
Kosmin, Barry A., 38-41, 44-45

Liebman, Charles S. and Saul Shipiro on dietary laws, 42

Maccabee, Judah, 82
Marriage, 7, 57, 93-104
  intermarriage, 38-39
  Judaic rite, 45-47
  marriage contract, 97-98
  sanctification of bride, 98
  Seven Blessings, 97-99
Meier, John P., *A Marginal Jew: Rethinking the Historical Jesus*, 24
Messianic hope, 60, 101, 106-7, 144
Michener, James, *The Source*, 162

New Year (Rosh Hashanah), 8-9,
    41, 53-56, 58-59

Orthodox Judaism, adult Jews'
    adherence to, 40-42, 44
Ozick, Cynthia, 162

Parallel Lives (Bullock), 24-25
Passover seder, family observance,
    7, 10, 41-44, 46-47, 51-52, 57,
    59, 61, 63-75, 123, 125, 155
Pentecost, 51, 59, 61

Qaddish, 60

Rashi, interpretation of marriage,
    95
Reconstructionist Judaism, 40, 125
Redemption, 7, 61
    Holocaust as Judaism of, 108-19,
        124-28, 148, 155-59
Reform Judaism, 35
    adult Jews' adherence to, 40-41
    Passover observance, 63-75
Religious beliefs and social practices
    of North American Jews, 13-
    15
    private and personal nature of,
        153-65
Revelation, 7
Rites of passage, 10, 12, 52

bar and bat mitzvah, 46, 59, 87-
    93
circumcision, 7, 17, 36, 45-47, 59,
    78-86, 109, 123
funerary rites, 46, 59-60, 103-7
marriage, 7, 38-39, 45-47, 57
Rosh Hashanah (New Year), 8-9,
    41, 53-56, 58-59

Sabbath observance, 53-54, 56, 59,
    61-62
Schachter, Lifsa, 81, 85
Shema, recitation of, 135-40, 146
Sociological examination of North
    American Jewish people, 30-48
State of Israel
    Holocaust as Judaism of
        redemption, 108-19, 157-61
    migration to, 132
Sukkot (Feast of Tabernacles), 8,
    51, 57-59, 61
Synagogue, attendance at, 51-62

Updike, John, 162

Wertheimer, Jack, 39-40, 44
World view
    Holocaust as Judaism of
        redemption, 108-19, 124-28,
        148, 155-59
    of North American Jewish
        people, 30-48

Yom Kippur (Day of Atonement),
    8-9, 41, 43-45, 47, 53-54, 56, 59

INDEX OF BIBLICAL
AND TALMUDIC
REFERENCES

◇

BIBLE

Genesis
3:5   95
18:18   85

Exodus
2:15   83

Leviticus
19:18   130

Numbers
15:37-41   138
25:11   83

Deuteronomy
6:5-9   137
11:13-21   138

1 Samuel
19:11   83
19:18   83

1 Kings
17:17-24   84
19:4   83
19:8   83
19:9-14   82
19:10-14   82

Psalms
15   130
113–118   70

Isaiah
33:6   129
33:25-26   131
56:1   131

Jeremiah
33:10-11   101

Hosea
12:12   83

Micah
6:8   131

Habakkuk
2:4   131

Malachi
1:23   84
3:1   84

Babylonian Talmud
Makkot
24a   131

Shabbat
31a   129–30